Michael Kellett

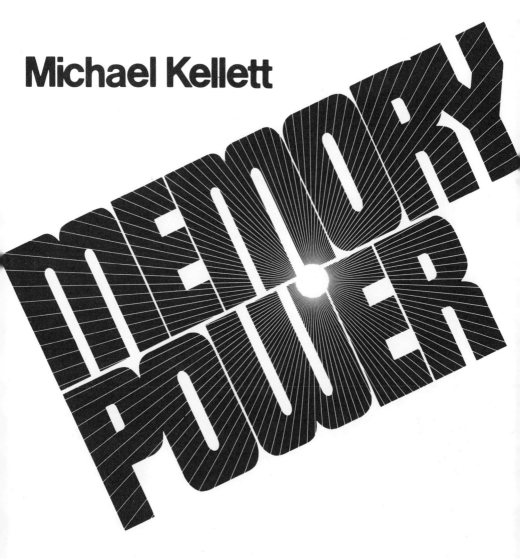

MEMORY POWER

Sterling Publishing Co., Inc. New York

Oak Tree Press Co., Ltd London & Sydney

To Bruce and Camille

Sources

Buchwald (1958) "New York Post"; New York, N.Y.

Link-Muzzey (1966) *Our American Republic*, Lexington, Massachusetts. Ginn & Co.

McWhirter, Norris (1981) *Guinness Book of World Records*, New York, N.Y. Sterling Publishing Co., Inc.

"Toward A National Energy Policy": Mobile Oil Corp. 1975. Questions contributed by Steve Alfano

The information on page 97 is according to the *Guinness Book of World Records*.

Library of Congress Cataloging in Publication Data

Kellett, Michael Cliff.
  Memory power.
  Includes index.
  1. Mnemonics. 2. Memory. I. Title.
BF385.K33   153.1'4   80-52338
ISBN 0-8069-0210-8
ISBN 0-8069-8946-7 (pbk.)
ISBN 0-8069-0211-6 (lib. bdg.)

Oak Tree ISBN 7061-2739-0

Copyright © 1980 by Michael Kellett
Published by Sterling Publishing Co., Inc.
Two Park Avenue, New York, N.Y. 10016
Distributed in Australia by Oak Tree Press Co., Ltd.,
P.O. Box 134, Brickfield Hill, Sydney 2000, N.S.W.
Distributed in the United Kingdom by Ward Lock Ltd.
116 Baker Street, London W.1
Manufactured in the United States of America
All rights reserved

contents

introduction

You are reading this book because you wish to improve your memory and your concentration. Fine! The subject of memory improvement, however, can mean different things to different people and it is important to first clarify your objectives.

How this book can help you

Memory and concentration are enhanced considerably when the individual has specific goals and purposes in mind. Therefore, let me offer some objectives which I believe should guide you as you read this book.

CONCENTRATION—How often have you been reading an article, listening to a lecture, or simply engaged in ordinary conversation, when you suddenly realize that your mind has wandered off the topic? You should try to find the causes of mind-wandering and cut down on this time-wasting activity.

IMPROVING THE ART OF COMMUNICATION—How often have you read an article or a chapter of a book, or listened to a lecture, *knowing* that you understood and would remember? You probably would have done well on a multiple choice or true-false test, but now the question is: "What did the author or lecturer say?" Recalling the information well enough to communicate it effectively to others is often more difficult than it should be. A thorough knowledge of the principle of mental organization will not only aid concentration and memory, it will also help improve reading speed, writing, speaking, and even the thinking process itself.

RECALL—How often have you been in the following situation: You are at a party and someone asks you to tell a joke. You must have heard dozens of appropriate anecdotes in your lifetime, but on this occasion you can't recall a single one. Then, when the party is over and all is quiet, while driving home, what happens? Several funny and appropriate anecdotes start flowing through your mind. It should be your objective, then, to learn techniques of memory that will enable you to remember when you want to, not only later on.

SPECIFIC AREAS OF MEMORY—You should also aim at learning how to cope with specific problem areas of memory such as recalling names and faces, and how to stop forgetting tasks and chores. You will learn how to remember numbers with seemingly incredible ability; how to remember the meaning of foreign words; how to remember a speech, and much, much more.

HUMAN UNDERSTANDING—Last but not least, you should strive to understand more about yourself and others. You are going to learn about the human mind. In a sense, this book shows how psychology can be applied to everyday life. Where memory is concerned, you shall see that human beings are subject to a consistent pattern of psychological principles. You always remember—or forget—for a reason. Knowing why people forget, what situations and conditions are likely to cause forgetting, will help you improve your memory. Moreover, that knowledge will enable you to make it possible for others to remember your words and your ideas.

What memory is and isn't

Memory is the re-creation of knowledge after a period of time during which you were not thinking of that knowledge. In other words, you are presented with certain information, some time passes during which your mind is occupied with other thoughts, and then you respond to some need to recall the information.

Some persons, incorrectly, will place the subject of memory alongside those of extrasensory perception, clairvoyance, mental telepathy, and other as-yet-unproven psychological phenomena. There is nothing mystical or supernatural about memory. Persons who have excellent memories possess no mental powers which are beyond those of the average individual. They simply are applying, consciously or not, the right technique to the right situation.

Can memory be improved?

People constantly say: "I have a poor memory," or "I have a good memory for numbers but a poor one for names." They speak of their ability to remember as if it had been arbitrarily bestowed upon them for the duration of their lives. Of course, a certain amount of inherent intelligence is a factor in dealing with information. Physical differences, however, are not responsible for the vastly different performances of individuals. It is more important to remember that memory ability can always be improved, regardless of one's physical characteristics.

Memory and concentration

Memory improvement cannot be classified as some separate type of mental functioning. In most instances, one cannot say that one technique improves memory while other techniques improve concentration or comprehension. The brain cells do not have certain areas for memory and other areas for learning. Memory and learning are intricately interwoven.

Even when using the proper terminology, mental functions can easily be confused. Has this ever happened to you? You are introduced to someone at a party or gathering but, when you later try to recall his/her name, you cannot. Why? Possibly because you never really learned the name in the first place. Perhaps you were busy thinking of some item of conversation and thus didn't learn the name. This common occurrence is usually described, incorrectly, as "forgetting," as if it were a problem of memory.

A student prepares for an examination by doing all the required reading on the subject, and if afterward he receives a grade of 80, we usually say that he learned eighty percent of the material. We could just as easily say that he *remembered* eighty percent of the material!

Any time that something is recalled, the end product is the result of a combination of several mental processes. Recalling depends as much on *how* you absorb, treat, and commit the information to memory, as it does on your ability to gather the information.

In the final analysis, memory is a kind of yardstick with which you measure how effective you are in any endeavor. It is the end product that counts, that is why memory is the major topic of discussion in this book. However, if you are eventually to recall successfully, *concentration* is the single most important factor whenever you are first presented with information. Nevertheless, as you will see, many of the same principles apply to *both* memory and concentration.

How to get the most out of this book

It is not enough to just read and understand the contents of this book. The object is to improve your ability, and one improves by thinking, reacting, and *doing*. You must be alert to the opportunities to apply these principles and techniques in your daily life. If, for example, you learn to read in a certain way, you should look for a way to apply what you have learned *every* time you read anything. Once you learn how to remember names, you should try to apply the technique on every occasion, whenever you meet someone—even people whose names may not be especially important to you. A good memory is a skill, and any skill improves with use and practice.

Whether or not you remember something depends to a major extent on you and how your mind treats information. The learning of several names in a short period of time would normally be quite difficult, especially during a meeting involving serious discussion and thoughts. Yet, you will most likely remember the names if you process the information correctly. Whether information is or is not processed correctly and effectively is determined by the presence or lack of certain mental factors.

The next section discusses these mental factors. Each factor is actually a principle of memory improvement. For example, the presence or lack of organization is a factor in memory and concentration. That you should look for organization in your material is a principle. You should keep in mind that this book discusses general principles. A principle is far-reaching and can be applied to a variety of problems and situations. Everyone has different problems concerning memory, but if you can get a clear idea of how these principles affect mental functioning, then the ideas offered can extend beyond the examples in these chapters. In other words, the reader with a good basic knowledge should apply these principles to a variety of life situations.

part I
memory:
the basic
principles

CHAPTER 1

use all your mental
powers

Principle No. 1 —
Use Faculties
Simultaneously

It is often disturbing to consider how little control we have over our minds. If you tell yourself to go to sleep because you must awaken early the next morning, it becomes ever so much more difficult to fall asleep. If you tell yourself to remember an important date or name, you are seemingly no more apt to remember than had you not bothered to tell yourself. If you pound the desk and tell yourself to concentrate, you lose concentration just the same. Psychologists have long recognized that we have less control over our conscious minds than is generally supposed. You cannot force yourself to concentrate. Your mind must be wooed into it.

Perhaps this perspective on the meaning of the word "concentration," will supply a concept which will be helpful in disciplining your mind. If a military commander masses all of his forces and armaments, and applies this mass to a vulnerable position along the enemy lines, is this concentration? Yes, it is. *Concentration* is the act of gathering, engaging, or utilizing as much of one's equipment as possible, and applying that arsenal within a limited and sharply defined sphere. Concentration is massing, then focusing.

By the same token, to concentrate effectively, what you must do is engage all of your resources, all of your mental faculties, and focus them on a single chain of thought or information.

You can woo your brain into concentrating by *involving* as many of your mental faculties as possible in the process of acquiring information. The mind deals with information basically in three ways: it reproduces and creates visual images; it reproduces sounds; and it recalls tactile or kinesthetic memories, in other words, touch or feelings.

These three faculties should all be utilized if possible when learning. Students will normally notice that taking notes improves concentration on a lecture. This is partly because the kinesthetic area of the brain is involved. If you are given facts in conversation, concentration and memory would be enhanced if you utilized the verbal faculty by repeating aloud or rephrasing the content in your own words. Last, if you can involve yourself physically in the learning process, a still better impression will be made in the brain. Who is more likely to remember the route correctly, the driver or the passenger? The driver, of course, because he/she is physically involved.

This book presents a number of other suggestions which will encourage a fuller use of your mental powers. The point here, though, is not that one faculty should be used instead of another, but rather that faculties used simultaneously make for better concentration and retention.

Of the three mental faculties, civilized man overwhelmingly favors verbalization as a source of thought, learning, and memory. If the average person is going to the store to buy several items, he/she will usually repeat "milk, eggs, bread," etc. to him/herself a few times. Most likely the images of the items will not be repeatedly produced, despite the fact that from the standpoint of memory, the images, rather than the words, will more likely be retained.

The value of using visual imagery is underrated. We were born with the propensity to learn by visualizing. Parents often discover that their one-year-old infant has learned how to feed him/herself. Does the infant say: "Okay, first I must stretch my arm, then grab the food, then bend my elbow, open my mouth, and place the food in?" More likely, the child has a visual picture of the correct procedure in his/her memory. If we recall our very first experiences, we will have one thing in common—that we all are remembering a picture. If you were presented with a photograph of a person for one second, and during that same second, the name was given, which memory would last longer, the name or the face? The face, of course.

Not only do you remember better when you process information visually rather than verbally, but concentration also improves. The mind is less likely to wander when it is occupied with visions rather than words.

In many instances, more than we realize, visualizing details and events is still the best way to remember. Visualization plays an important role in many areas of memory improvement. You can try some exercises designed to start you thinking in visual terms, to give practice in visualizing, and to show some *applications* of this principle. First, though, here are a few more suggestions.

When visualizing, try to:
1. Visualize clearly, and in vivid color. Colorful images are much easier to see and recall than drab ones.
2. Exaggerate. Tall-tales are more interesting and easier to remember than simple, factual stories. You will remember better when you enlarge things in your mind.
3. Picture in three dimensions. Your mind's eye is not as limited as a TV or movie screen. It can imagine in three dimensions, thereby making the images more lifelike. Don't worry about taking up space in your mind.
4. Imagine movement and action. We tend to visualize in still pictures. The more movement in your mental picture, the better you will remember it.

The following exercises are designed to provide practice in visualizing. Perhaps you will also notice some applications. Read the following passage, and then, strictly from memory, try to draw the directions in a very rough sketch. One point before you start. If you try to remember in the usual way, by just repeating the words to yourself, you won't stand a chance. The only way to do this efficiently is to visualize making the turns, walking through the park, etc.

VISUALIZATION EXERCISE #1

Go straight until you come to a fork in the road. Then turn right and travel to the second four-way stop. Then turn left and keep going until you come to a tunnel. Make your first left after you get out of the tunnel. Then go past two traffic lights and you should see a monument on the right-hand side. You want the building that is before the monument.

Now try to reproduce the directions. How did you do? Go back to the paragraph now and check your diagram. See how many items you can recall in the next exercise. Have fun! It is not meant to be easy.

VISUALIZATION EXERCISE #2

The selection below is an imaginary stage setting. (Downstage means toward the audience; upstage means toward the rear of the stage. Right and left mean the right and left of the audience as it looks toward the stage.) Read the directions and then, without referring to them again, draw a rough stage setting. It is not necessary to draw the articles mentioned, merely indicate them.

In the right wall are two large casement windows. In the left wall is a large fireplace (downstage) and a door (upstage) leading to the dining room. Above the mantel is a large oil painting. In the center of the back wall is a double French door.

Between the windows at the right are a desk and chair. A couch, with a small table in front of it, is to the right of the desk. Against the right of the back wall stands a grandfather clock, and in the right corner is a table with a lamp.

In front of the fireplace is a love seat. Two large arm-chairs, with a small table between them, occupy the left side of the stage. Against the left side of the back wall is a chest and at its right a low table with a lamp.

Principle No. 2 — Ego Involvement

Since we remember things that happen to us better than what happens to others, the principle of ego involvement is very important. When you read something, create an experience for yourself. Make yourself the central figure that everything revolves around.

Below is a passage to commit to memory. Utilize the ego-involvement principle. If you put yourself in this passage and visualize everything in motion, in three dimensions and living color, you will be surprised at how easy it is.

VENUS OBSERVED

NASA's Mariner II Spacecraft flew past Venus at a distance of 21,648 miles, giving man his first relatively close-up observation of

Earth's mysterious planetary neighbor. This Venus fly-by climaxed an epic flight experiment that significantly advanced the world's knowledge about Venus and about interplanetary space, and contributed to planning for man's eventual journey to the Moon and to other planets.

The Mariner observations, together with radar and optical studies made from Earth, should cause man to discard any romantic conception that may have persisted of Venus as being a place with Earth-like qualities. Mariner found that the temperatures of Venus may be as hot as 800° F. This temperature, hot enough to melt lead, eliminated the possibility of life like that which exists on Earth.

Radar studies supply evidence that Venus rotates once each 225 Earth days while orbiting the Sun in the same time period. Thus, every day or night on Venus lasts about 112½ Earth days, or half the planet's rotational period. Presumably, the Venusian clouds screen out most of the sunlight, keeping that hemisphere in twilight.

The long Venusian day and night would be expected to make the side of the planet facing the Sun become quite hot and the other become cold. Mariner, however, did not find any appreciable difference in temperature, so the dense atmosphere must circulate vast quantities of heat from the day side to the night side.

Radar studies also suggest that Venus rotates backwards with respect to Earth and other planets of the solar system, except Uranus and perhaps Pluto. Thus, on Venus, the Sun rises in the West and sets in the East.

If you really created an experience for yourself, it will be a long time before you forget these facts about Venus.

Now imagine this: You are lost and stop at a gas station for directions. The attendant says, "Oh sure, no problem . . . just go up three blocks, then turn right and go straight for six traffic lights. Now turn left. You will come to a fork, bear right and go over a bridge. Take your first right after the bridge. Then go two blocks, make a left and you'll see it on your left-hand side. You can't miss it."

You know what you would usually say to yourself under this condition: "I'll go up the three blocks, turn right, and ask someone else." Well, now you know how to do it. Put yourself in an imaginary driver's seat as the directions are given, see yourself in action turning the wheel, create the whole experience, and you will remember your experience.

Convert abstract to concrete

It is not always possible to visualize information. When dealing in concrete terms, as with objects and places, there is no problem. Many things, however, cannot be pictured. Concepts, numbers, and abstract words such as "faith," "justice," etc. cannot be dealt with easily. Nevertheless, you can visualize abstractions if you convert the abstract into concrete terms. Follow this example:

The touch-tone telephone has numbers in the following positions:

$$1 \quad 2 \quad 3$$
$$4 \quad 5 \quad 6$$
$$7 \quad 8 \quad 9$$
$$0$$

Suppose the last four digits of a number you wished to remember are 3749. You could convert this into the concrete figure below, which is much easier to remember than four numbers in exact order. (To help remember the order, you would imagine *yourself* constructing the figure.)

Notice that doing things like this entails one more mental operation. After you recall the symbol you must convert it back into numbers, but that should be very easy in this case, since the numbers hardly change position.

Charts and graphs can often be converted to concrete symbols or objects. So can abstract words, as Chapter 6 will show.

Principle No. 3 — Use Your Emotions

Along with your personal involvement, also try to bring in your emotions and feelings. Emotional episodes are permanently retained in your memory storage. Those who are old enough to have been shocked by the death of President Kennedy can still recall not only the actual learning of the tragedy but the activity they were engaged in at that time, as well as the time of day and the surrounding environment.

Of course, it is unlikely that you would be able to, or would desire to, stimulate this type of emotional reaction. Nevertheless, it is possible to induce milder emotional states by becoming more personally involved in your reading and listening.

Principle No. 4 —
Use the Sound of
Your Voice

It is absolutely amazing how one can be affected by the sound of one's own voice. Numerous interesting studies have been made of people participating in debates. Individuals were randomly selected and given a viewpoint to defend. Later observation showed that after the debate, personal views had shifted toward the position they had been assigned to advocate.

It may sound crazy, but before starting to read, simply stating out loud something such as, "I want to learn how the new machine works," does enhance interest, concentration, retention, and motivation. Your brain listens to, and remembers, the sound of your own voice. How often have you asked a friend to remind you to do something? Your friend forgets, but you remember.

You can solve the problem of forgetting where you have placed objects, to a large extent, through the use of the voice. Verbal declarations such as "I am now placing the voucher in the upper right-hand drawer," or "I am now placing the receipt in the glove compartment," will do wonders for recall. Be sure to actually *say* it. Don't just "think it."

Vocalizing should be employed whenever possible. A business schedule can often be planned and later remembered while driving to work in the morning, if the planning is done out loud. If it is a rainy or foggy morning, you may wish to turn your lights on. To avoid the possibility of leaving the car with lights still on, vocalize loud and clear, "I have just turned my lights on. I shall turn off my lights as soon as I turn off the motor." Say it with feeling.

An important characteristic of man as a social animal is the tendency to communicate with others. Class discussions are usually more fun than lectures or reading because conversation is involved. Speech can so readily transform drudgery into interest. The more you talk in class, and the more you discuss subjects with others outside of class, the greater your interest and retention will be.

Principle No. 5 —
Your Own Actions

We do many things either haphazardly or habitually, without consciously being aware of our actions. Yet, if you make a conscious effort to notice your physical movements, you can make an extremely effective impression on your mental mechanism. People walk, drive, and put things away without giving attention to their activities. You should become aware of the physical activity that accompanies something you want to remember. Later on, when you want to recall, you can start memories flowing back by first recalling your physical movements.

Part II has several examples which utilize this principle. An important point to mention here, though, is that not only can you enhance memory by directing attention to the actual physical movement, but also *imagining* your physical action will help too. Suppose a woman is introduced and her name is Pat. It might be rather inappropriate to pat her, but clearly imagining yourself doing that will be almost as good.

CHAPTER 2

how thoughts become connected

Principle No. 6 — The Principle of Association

Any thought, action, statement, word, or whatever, can trigger another related memory. When you recall what you had for dinner last night, that may remind you of something someone said at dinner, which may recall the memory of the music that was playing, which may evoke an incident that occurred 15 years ago, and this can go on and on. Impressions are not stored away in an isolated state. Memories become connected so that one tends to remind you of another. It would then make sense to say that the more connections, or associations, that an idea has, the more easily remembered the idea will be. Memory improvement, then, depends largely on increasing the closeness and number of associations.

In elementary school, some simple associations may have been used to aid memory. *Teacher* is a word that often causes trouble, but when *teach* is associated with *each*, which is seldom misspelled, the difficulty is removed. *There* and *their* are two words whose spelling often causes confusion, but it is overcome when *there* is associated with *where* and *here* and *their* with *her*, *your*, *our*, etc. *Sight*, *site*, and *cite* are also stumbling blocks in spelling, but *sight* can be associated with *light* and *night*, *site* with *situation*, and *cite* with *recite*.

Ideas are connected in many ways. They can be associated because they occur at the same time or in the same place. For example: fork and spoon. Things may be associated by a similarity in meaning, such as coat and jacket, or by similar sounds such as might and fight. Opposites such as fat and thin can easily be associated. Whole and part relationships work, such as sink and kitchen. There are also associations that work simply because the items belong to the same classification, such as dolphin and porpoise.

Mnemonic associations

The problem with remembering many facts is that often they have no relation to each other which can be used for association. There is absolutely nothing in the normal course of reasoning to link the number 14 or the fourteenth President of the United States with the name Franklin Pierce. Nor is there anything to link the French word "venir" with its meaning, "to go." There are ways, however, in which you can create an association when none apparently exists. The devices or systems used for this are called *mnemonics*.

Cues

Whenever an association is used in memory, one idea serves to recall another. The idea or environmental object that brings forth the desired response is called the *cue.* Cues may come from the environment or from inner mental representations. In other words when someone says "ten," the desired response may be "toes." Sometimes it is desirable for the association to be able to work backwards. Someone may call out the word "toes" and "ten" is the desired response. In this slightly more difficult instance, "toes" acts as the cue. This is called a *backward association.*

Information may be associated visually or verbally. Here is an illustration of the association technique as it applies to the learning of foreign words: The word "hola" in Spanish means "hello." You can easily recognize a connection here as the sounds are similar, so just a little repetition of the association will most likely assure retention. Now suppose you come to "fungia," which means "mushroom." It would be harder to connect these two, but once you observe that "fungia" sounds like "fungus," you can deal with the information better. Note that a series of connections actually will cause recall. "Fungia" reminds you of "fungus" which reminds you of "mushroom." There are three links here; there can be several links in the series. The number doesn't affect memory, as the brain can process information with amazing rapidity. The important factor is the closeness of the association.

In the first example, the association was actually contained in the information given. In the second, you had to be somewhat creative, but recognized an association that did exist. Sometimes you must use your creativity and make connections. This entails concentrating on a mnemonic association. You can do this verbally by getting information together in the form of a sentence. You want to learn that "gato" means "cat" so you can form the sentence, "I 'gato' a new 'cat'." Repeat the sentence a few times and the meaning will stick. Later on, when searching for the translation for "cat," you would remember the sentence and retrieve the memory.

Visual associations

You can also connect information by getting two ideas together in the same mental picture. To remember that the French word for apple is "pomme," you might visualize yourself being pummeled by apples.

Visual associations, though tending to be ludicrous at times, are usually more effective than verbal associations. The visual should be used whenever possible. However, when dealing with abstract words or ideas such as "truth," "faith," etc., verbal associations will normally be easier.

The technique of chaining

One key value of associations is that one association can always be chained to another, so that any number of ideas can be triggered by one initial thought. Suppose, for example, you wished to memorize all the principles of memory improvement given thus far, in exact order. Select cues and place each cue in a story. You start the story chain with yourself as often as possible and connect that image to a cue for the subject. So picture yourself as a prince (cue for basic principles), you are attending a faculty meeting (see the title of the first principle), you imagine that you hear a voice (visualization followed by the vocalizing principle) which is a call for action (number four), but first you reach for an aspirin (cue for association). You may try to continue your story and remember all the principles. You will be amazed at the efficiency of this technique.

Letter associations

One of the oldest and most effective methods of association is to use the first letter of key words, statements, or facts, and combine them into a word or phrase. The word may be a cue for a list of factors, events, etc., pertaining to a particular subject. To remember the names of the five Great Lakes, you might think of "HOMES" (for Huron, Ontario, Michigan, Erie, and Superior). You can also make up a sentence with the first letter of each word of the sentence being the same as the first letter of each thing you want to remember.

Letter associations are generally easier and more quickly committed to memory than visual story chains, although the latter are usually more effective over long intervals. The former is most suitable for the individual who must quickly jot down points to make, or must prepare for a quick speech.

Letter associations are quite effective, but you must recognize that they have a weak spot. You will usually be able to remember your "word" or sequence of letters alright, but it is possible to forget the word that the letter is supposed to represent. Recognizing this, and consequently spending a little extra time reviewing and reciting the connections, should solve the problem.

Principle No. 7 —
Organization

Assume that you are asked to remember these words in order: "the," "wanted," "on," "table," "room." You would most likely have to repeat them to yourself a few times to remember them, but if you add a few more words you get: "the," "books," "you," "wanted," "are," "on," "the," "table," "in," "that," "room." You can remember the second list more easily. Although there are more words, they fit into a pattern. They are organized. If you were to add "pillow" or "nut" to the list they would be more difficult to remember because they do not fit into the structure. You could, however, add "dining" in front of "room" and it would easily be remembered. You can see that the amount of information to be learned is not the crucial factor in determining whether something will be easily remembered. The *degree of organization* is more important.

If you were asked to go to the store for celery, carrots, chopped meat, milk, and eggs without writing the items down, you would normally review the list several times. Just as you were leaving for the store, suppose someone said that those items were unnecessary and another list was given instead.

Now the list reads: bread, raisins, applesauce, and chicken. Naturally the mind would have difficulty remembering, and could mix up one list with the other. However, more information could be added in a less harmful way. You could make the list read:

> *a loaf of* bread
> *a box of* raisins
> *a jar of* applesauce
> *two pounds of* chicken

The second addition of facts is only slightly more difficult to remember. The items relate. They have organization.

Organization affects learning

Memories are located in complex, interwoven systems and structures. All knowledge must find some other knowledge to relate to. If you cannot find a thought or group of thoughts which a new piece of knowledge can relate to, that new knowledge will usually be discarded. That is why nonsense words such as "blim," or "plurg," would be far more difficult to remember than a list of meaningful, familiar words. For this reason a new subject should be approached with the aim of learning the most basic concepts first— to provide a base of knowledge for the following information.

Individuals require different periods of time to absorb different signals, depending upon the input itself, and the unique background of the individual. As an example, if you are told that a certain kind of rock is called "shale," the acquisition of this fact, for most people, would require a few moments of sustained concentration and repetition. This will definitely not, however, be necessary for someone who has a background in geology and can then relate the new knowledge to prior knowledge. On the other hand, if you were told for the first time that the world is round, you would need no repetition. The thought, because it is extremely significant and affects so many concepts of nature, the universe, and yourself, would fit into many existing thought structures.

Psychological studies on the development of attitudes have shown that people will remember more of the points in an argument if the argument agrees with their own feelings on the subject. A group of students was divided into two groups, those considered pro-Communist and those anti-Communist. After hearing two speeches, one supporting and one antagonistic to Communism, the students were asked questions. It was found that each group remembered distinctly more of the speech which accorded with its own views. This can be explained in terms of motivation and interest, both of which influence attention. It can also be explained in terms of organization. Each student remembered more of the speech which fit into his/her nicely organized concepts and supporting principles. Each remembered the new messages that fit more easily into an established pattern.

Finding and creating organization

Material is both easier to concentrate on as well as easier to recall if it is organized. However, a large part of the process depends upon how you perceive your material. It is a two-way street. When a person can *perceive* or recognize the relationships between things, memory is enhanced. Sometimes material is presented in a poor way but the reader or listener is motivated enough to make sense out of the material, and it is then retained. At other times, an author works to exhaustion to present the material in an organized manner, but the reader fails to pay heed to his/her efforts, and mind-wandering or poor comprehension results.

Telephone numbers usually consist of disorganized data, but if you perceive relationships between the numbers, memory will be enhanced. Taking the number 482-2561, notice how multiples of the number 2 figure in the organization of the exchange and 7 (2 + 5 and 6 + 1) relates to the numbers on the right. You could find other relationships as well, and the more you do, the greater will be the chances of retention. Of course there are other ways to remember telephone numbers. They will be covered later, but if you try remembering numbers by finding relationships, you will gain a good understanding of the principle of organization.

Thought structure in daily communication

Imagine yourself walking into a supermarket and meeting your friend, Jane. After some casual talk she asks if you will be seeing Barbara, a mutual friend. You reply that you will, and Jane asks you to relay this message: "Please tell Barbara that I can't play tennis tomorrow. According to the weather report we are due to have a storm. I wonder if we'll go without electricity. Besides, I hit my arm on the car door and strained a muscle. I thought I broke it! I wonder how long it will take to heal."

Now, you would not wish to remember this message word for word. You most likely would transmit this message in synopsis.

Perhaps you would say to Barbara, "Jane had a very important message to give you. She wanted me to tell you that she was wondering if we'll have no electricity." Needless to say, that would not be a very good relay of the message. The message could actually take the form of a structure:

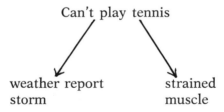

Jane's having thought that the arm was broken is a detail, it is meaningless and forgotten easily unless associated with a main idea.

Any time a body of information is communicated, you must realize that it has a structure or organization. Try not to remember a bunch of isolated facts, or else mind-wandering will result. Just the act of searching for organization in material enhances overall concentration.

We can all do fairly well in remembering everyday conversation and ideas. However, when information is in printed form, which is usually well structured and organized, the structure falls apart. Most people make no effort to locate the main idea.

Usually we accord each statement equal weight. Most students can answer questions about single facts but are totally lost when asked, "What was the chapter about?"

People who aren't students are no better than students. When listening to a political speech they tend to remember a "choice" line about some controversial issue rather than the main theme of the speech. Although many of us can relate the beginning or end of the Gettysburg Address, very few can ever tell us the main theme that Lincoln was trying to get across.

Memory for a practical purpose

There are a couple of implications to be drawn from what this section has discussed. First, it becomes necessary to clarify your concept of the word "memory" as it pertains to such things as speeches, chapters, articles, etc. Memory is recalling thoughts, not words. What if you could go back in time and ask someone of the 19th century if he/she remembers the Gettysburg Address? Person "A" says, "Yes, I remember it as if it were yesterday. I remember he said that 'four score and seven years ago our forefathers brought forth this nation,' and that . . . oh yes, 'that we could not consecrate or hallow this ground,' and the best part of all . . . 'the world will little note, nor long remember what we say here, but it can never forget what they did here,' and last, 'that this nation was of the people, for the people, and by the people'." Person "B" says, "I don't remember the exact words, but he said that the nation was founded on great moral principles and that the people must be determined not to let it perish." Of the two, only "B" can claim to have remembered the speech. Despite being unable to furnish a flood of information, he/she has conveyed the essentials. Thus you may now take a more practical view of normal reading memory. You remember if you can recall the message correctly. You remember better if you can recall the general theme plus the main ideas, and all the supporting facts and details. You should always recognize priorities in committing ideas to memory.

Implications for recall

The second implication you can draw by referring to "B's" memory of the Gettysburg Address is that certain statements are more important than others. The important statements remind us of other statements or facts that are related to them. The key to memory often lies in finding that one starting point or idea that will trigger other related memories.

Statements are capable of triggering other information, but the effectiveness of any statement depends on its relative position in the total scheme. To remember that Jane said, "I wonder if we'll have no electricity" will be of less help in recall than remembering the main idea of the message. If you first remember the main theme, that she can't play tennis tomorrow, the logical recollection of why she can't play would more than likely come to mind. These concepts will be particularly important when discussing methods of improving concentration and memory for reading.

Here is a summary of the organization principle:

1. You remember and concentrate better when things are presented in a pattern, relationship, structure, etc.
2. New information will be more easily absorbed if the incoming knowledge relates to already existing thought or knowledge.
3. In receiving disorganized data, just the act of finding and creating relationships enhances memory and concentration.
4. Organization entails recognizing priorities when you are acquiring information. This recognition not only helps concentration, but also will facilitate recall of the information in a manner that will aid communication.

CHAPTER 3

directing the conscious mind

Principle No. 8 —
Select and Discriminate

You have seen that certain ideas contain considerably more information than others. You have also seen that certain ideas, when properly organized, will enable you to recall related ideas. It becomes apparent, then, that words and sentences vary tremendously in value. They may take up equal space on paper, but should not take up equal space in your mind. Some ideas demand intense attention, while some are to be virtually ignored.

Memory is always selective. If you are not convinced, ask yourself these questions. How many times have you seen a $20.00 bill? Then, whose picture is on it? What does he look like? How many times have you picked up the telephone receiver and dialed the letter F? In the same dial hole, there is a number. What is that number? If these questions are difficult, it is because the face and the number were not selected for special attention; certainly not because you were unavailed of the experiences of seeing a telephone dial and a $20.00 bill!

Discrimination is quite possibly the most important principle in this book. Practically any situation involving memory requires, as an early step, the mental operation of deciding what stands out, is unusual, or is most important about whatever it is that is to be remembered. No matter what the situation, just going through the mental acts of selecting certain ideas or objects as being more important helps concentration and memory.

Imagine that you are hurriedly parking your car at the airport, and you know that you might forget where you parked your car when you return. Telling yourself that the car is in row 23, position H, is a lot better than just hurrying off. However, if you can pick out some landmark, perhaps a flagpole, statue—anything permanent—and note where the car is in relation to your selection, you will remember. To recall, you will first ask yourself what you picked out and your selection will always come back. Recall of the location of the desired object, the car in this case, will follow almost immediately. So much of memory improvement involves the crucial act of finding that first starting point that will trigger other memories. A prior selection can usually be that starting point.

Extracting concepts

Organization and discrimination can be utilized to commit certain things to memory by extracting a principle or concept, or a rule from a body of information. In memorizing the amendments to the Constitution, it is helpful to note consistencies such as: Amendments five through eight are about the court and jury system, nine through 11 deal with elections, etc. Recognizing that all the main points of some speeches begin with a question would be another example. If a rule can be extracted, it can be quite helpful even if there are some exceptions. You may recall the rule "*i* before *e* except after *c*" helped you remember the correct vowel position in spelling. There are innumerable instances where the noting of common properties can enhance retention. The key is to be alert and recognize them.

The unique and unusual aid memory

Suppose you are to recall the interiors of automobiles. Four are blue, and one is red. Which would you remember most easily? Yes, even the interior of the red car would be remembered more quickly. You remember more easily not only that which stands out or is unusual, but you are also more likely to recall that which is associated with it. There are a couple of implications here. One: something may not be unusual or different, but if you *find* something that is extraordinary, you will remember better. Two: if you are imagining an association, it would help to create something truly unusual and perhaps absurd. You will be more likely to remember that association. This concept has many applications.

Principle No. 9 —
Put Things in Classes
and Categories

Now suppose you are asked to remember these nine words in any order: "pillow," "quilt," "car," "movie," "train," "play," "mattress," "carnival," and "plane." Give these words a heading:

Things going on a bed	Entertainment	Transportation
mattress	movie	car
pillow	play	plane
quilt	carnival	train

The second group is now easier to remember because you have *classified* your material. In a sense, you have reduced the number of things to memorize from nine to three. When later on you wish to recall, you need only remember the heading "Entertainment" for the three words associated with it to follow.

Here is the principle: the smaller the unit or category that the mind deals with, the more effective the mind will be. Look at how this works together with the last principle, discrimination.

A lieutenant in the fire department had just been transferred and his first job was to memorize the location and fastest route to any place in the new district. After all, it would be sort of embarrassing to have to consult a map with the fire blazing. There were a great many different streets and it was quite confusing. Yet the job was made infinitely easier by doing the following. First, he divided the district into six equally sized areas. Next, he selected one landmark from each of the areas, one place which he would instantly know how to get to, and which was located near the center of each area. From there he remembered each street in relation to the landmark in that area. That was a lot easier than remembering each street in relation to the fire station. Common sense? Yes, but just the same do not miss the opportunities to divide, classify, or categorize.

Principle No. 10 — Long- and Short-Range Goals

A goal is a measurable level of performance toward which you can strive. Goals may be long or short range. Examples of goals are: finishing a race, obtaining a degree, or losing 10 pounds.

Goal-setting is important in a great variety of fields. A number of books have been written dealing with such diverse subjects as how to: succeed, think, get rich, be happy, as well as many others. One of the central themes throughout many of these books is the value in working toward a goal and then completing what you have started.

The student who expects to be a doctor, teacher, or engineer has a more favorable opportunity for becoming interested in his/her work than does the one who has not the slightest idea as to what he/she is going to do. The same holds true for anyone of any age. Once you set up that major life objective, the intermediate steps become much more interesting and therefore easier to concentrate on, because they are clearly seen as steps leading toward a desired goal.

Memory and organization are intricately related, as you have seen. Goal-setting is related to organization in a larger sense, and thus, also related to memory. It is no coincidence that people who are extremely forgetful will also tend to describe themselves as being disorganized in everyday affairs. Such people see no continuity in their lives. Little things to be done are not regarded as having a purpose. The chores are not performed with an ultimate goal in mind. A typical example is the college student who habitually forgets to do his assignments. He swears that his actions were unintentional, and that he would have done it if only he had remembered. Usually the problem lies in the student's candid admission that he does not know why he is going to school or what he wants to become after graduation.

Setting short-range goals

It is a well known fact that a person will concentrate better when he/she has a goal in mind. What is somewhat less well known is that concentration and effort increase as a person comes closer to attaining the goal. An exhausted cross-country runner often gets a "second wind" as the finish line finally comes into view.

If you have, say, 50 pages to read, this may appear as quite a chore. However, if you were to divide the assignment into smaller parts, you could set more goals for yourself. In so doing, you would create more finish lines. You would attain more levels of satisfaction and you would always be close to attaining a goal. Books and organized material are usually divided into sections, chapters, titles, and often subtitles, and you can usually set short-range reading goals in accordance with the breakdown.

Finish what you have started

Intensity of interference is a factor in forgetting. Yet, intensity is really dependent upon the psychological makeup of the individual. The person who is bothered by worries, or who is constantly troubled by things in the back of his/her mind, will bring these worries along to new and unrelated situations. His/her own state of mind will cause each situation to be more interfering than normal. Tension can be avoided, to a large extent, by completing what one has started. Tasks and projects should be dealt with one at a time.

A characteristic of little projects, tasks, and obligations is that they are quite vulnerable to interruptions by other, supposedly more important, matters. Some people are so often putting things aside for other matters that they never get anything done. They may get nothing done, but they sure do it fast. Once you form any goal, particularly one requiring mental energy, such as doing an assignment or writing a business letter, you should complete it. Failure to complete goals results not only in an inefficient use of time, but also creates a state of tension which will tend to hamper and diminish your ability to perform other tasks. Failure to complete something the night before will render you more susceptible to distraction and forgetfulness the next morning. Completion, on the other hand, carries with it a measure of satisfaction which reduces tension and tends to raise your level of performance in future tasks.

Principle No. 11 — Prepare Mentally

You will concentrate better when the brain knows, or has an idea or belief, about what will be presented to it. If you are a student and unable to find time to do your assigned reading, never discard the assignment completely. Spending just a few minutes to gain an overview of the topic to be discussed in class will be of great help. If the mind is suddenly hit with new material, it will tend toward drifting and escapism. Any good lawyer fully realizes the value in anticipating the opponent's presentation. Think, anticipate, and visualize beforehand.

When the brain is prepared for a future situation, it will function better, not only as concerns memory, but in other psychological areas as well. Alvin Toffler, in his book *Future Shock*, shows that the anticipation of future events will help to reduce stress and its consequent harm to the body.

This principle relates to several other suggestions in this book: goal-setting, imagining a use, generating thoughts, and ascertaining the difficulty of the recall situation. Because this principle is so important, I have decided to treat it separately.

Has something like the following ever happened to you? You are a student in class, you did your homework and know the material, but when the teacher suddenly asks you a question, you are at a loss for words.

Recall problems come when information is needed urgently and unexpectedly. If you prepare and anticipate for tense situations beforehand, the situation will be less drastic as far as memory is concerned.

The speaker at a business meeting can prepare by imagining the entire situation: he pictures difficult questions being asked in rapid succession, and himself confidently answering each one.

Principle No. 12 — The "Thought" Principle

Some very interesting observations of memory development can be made by watching young children. The same factors that cause variations in adult memory performances also apply to children. Several years ago my wife, myself, and my son (who was not yet two at the time) were eating dinner at a friend's house. The dessert consisted of warm delicious brownies, to which the boy instantly took a liking. When finished with his portion, he desired more but did not know how to ask for it, as he had not been taught the name of what he had eaten.

I became aware of his predicament when I felt him tugging on my arm and saying, "more chawkit bwed?" while pointing to the far end of the table. I did not know what he wanted at first. Finally, it dawned on me. I said, "Oh, chocolate bread! Yes, that makes sense," and handed him another brownie. It wasn't until at least five months later that we had brownies again. Five months is an extremely long time in the life of a two-year-old. Yet when he saw the brownies, he immediately exclaimed with glee, "oooo, chawkit bwed." He had not forgotten, a truly unusual feat for a child his age.

A person's natural ability to remember, from a physiological standpoint, increases gradually until the age of about sixteen. Nevertheless, you can learn from this incident and see how the principles apply.

Had I told the child that the substance was called "brownies," he most likely would not have remembered over the interval. He remembered "chawkit bwed" because this term had meaning for him. It was not an arbitrary designation. It fit neatly into his own limited, but working, memory structures. It had organization. Yet, of equal importance, he remembered because it was his own thought, his own construction. We are all able to remember our own thoughts and our own experiences far better than anyone else's. Once you have obtained a solution to a problem as a result of your own conscious processes, you do not easily forget it.

Locations of objects can be recalled if you think before putting something down. Constructing a reason *why* an item ought to be placed in a certain drawer, as opposed to another, will result in more efficient recall. Often the reason, the thought, will be recalled first. That will lead to the recollection of having placed the object in that particular drawer. Any time a judgment or decision is made, the mind will tend to remember that mental operation. This will lead to other recollections.

CHAPTER 4

the mental and physical factors

Some people will be able to memorize a poem or song or even a speech without having the vaguest notion of its meaning. We can all recall from our elementary school days how we would remember poems by rote, often without having the vaguest idea of their meaning or underlying thought. You could still succeed at this task, of course, if you could duplicate the motivation. Chances are that you could not. Meaning, use, and understanding take on more and more importance as we grow older.

When something has meaning, is understood, and makes sense, it is easier to remember. Nonsense syllables like "gub," "bla," "pra," etc., are more quickly forgotten than familiar words. Mathematical formulas are retained longer if the person knows how the formula is devised as well as how to use it.

Factors influencing comprehension

When things make sense, when you comprehend meanings, structures, and reasons for things being a particular way, learning and memory are enhanced. You may recall in geometry the formula for the area of a right triangle is found by multiplying the base by the height and dividing by two. Remembering this formula by itself is no monumental feat, but when it is placed alongside other formulas for finding areas of rectangles, circles, other triangles, and parallelograms, as well as formulas for circumferences and volumes, the list can cause considerable interference. If, however, the elementary concept of base times height of a rectangle is understood, the formula for the area of a triangle becomes far more comprehensible. When it is explained that any right triangle is actually half of a rectangle you can see the relationship, helping you to understand why the area of a right triangle is half the base times the height. The student who gains meaning in this manner will not forget.

There are a great many factors, mental, emotional, and environmental, entering into your level of comprehension. You may fail to understand a paragraph or chapter for a number of complicated reasons. To do true justice to this topic would require a book in itself. Nevertheless, because comprehension is an extremely important influence on learning and retention, two factors will be discussed briefly.

Prior knowledge

The knowledge a person brings with him/her to a subject is probably the single most important factor in comprehension. Prior knowledge is sometimes necessary as a prerequisite for the acquisition of new knowledge. Such is the case in learning to repair a television. One could hardly embark on such a venture without a firm foundation in basic electronics.

In most liberal arts courses, prior knowledge is not essential for basic understanding, yet, even in these subjects, it definitely does affect comprehension. All things being equal, someone who has a fair background in economics will be better able to comprehend a selection about Adam Smith than one who does not, even if the former had never studied Smith previously. This is because he/she already has some concepts to which the new information can relate. Other aspects of economics will take on more meaning as a result of the new knowledge, and the new information will in turn be affected by the old.

Memory and comprehension

You can see that organized structures in memory behave like sponges. The larger they become, the more new concepts that can be absorbed. Memory depends to some extent on comprehension, and comprehension, in turn, depends on memory.

Memories, however, are not always used to the best advantage in helping to admit new knowledge. Memories may lie dormant and be only slightly useful, on a subconscious level, or they may be consciously awakened. Two people may conceivably possess the same amount of knowledge about a subject, but the person who recalls more of that knowledge beforehand will have an advantage.

It thus becomes clear that before starting a new topic or subject, the student should try to recall as much as possible. Anything that may relate to the subject may be helpful. In this way, the learner prepares to assimilate the new information.

Principle No. 14 — The Principle of Review

The more the brain deals with any given information, the more permanent the mental impression that will be made, and the more surely the information will be recalled. Different methods of review will be discussed.

Repetition versus recitation

It is important, at this point, to realize that there are basically only two forms of review. You can repeat the procedure that was followed to learn the material. In other words, you can listen to the information again or repeat the reading of a passage. This is the most common memory technique used, though not the most efficient. I hope that by now you are using other methods to commit information to memory. You can also recite, in other words, try to reproduce the material from your own memory. All things being equal, *recitation is far superior to repetition, as an aid to memory.* The more recitation, the greater will be the recall. Numerous experiments comparing people and their ability to recall data have shown that time spent in reciting details will probably result in far superior recall, than if an equal amount of time is spent in simply rereading the details.

Exercise versus usage

It is well known that all human anatomical structures can change as a result of environmental demands. A man who works hard as a laborer for years, and then receives a promotion to a desk job, will lose size and strength in his muscles if he does not continue to exercise. There is no reason why brain cells should be different. A cell will lose some of its characteristics if it is not used, and forgetting will occur.

Usage and exercise are distinct. If a woman lifts an ax repeatedly to chop wood for the fire, she is using her muscles. If she uses the same muscles to lift weights, she is exercising. If a student repeats foreign phrases to himself to prepare for a test, he is exercising. If he goes to the foreign country, he will use the phrases to communicate.

Usage is the best aid to retention. A very bright college student may have some difficulty remembering principles of insurance or investment in an economics course. Yet, a young married man of average intelligence, after actually applying the principles in his financial decisions, will better retain his knowledge. This is especially true if he becomes aware of the need to alter his finances, should his personal conditions change.

Imagine a use

You do not need an immediate use for information in order to employ the principle of usage. You can, and always should, imagine situations in which an item of information can be used. Upon hearing an anecdote, you should think of times and places for which the anecdote would be appropriate. If you uncover something of interest, imagine yourself properly communicating the information to others who share the interest. If you have extracted an interesting piece of information from reading, or if you have come up with a thought yourself, *imagine conversation that would relate to the information.* Later, when such conversation arises, you will be much more likely to recall the information.

Use your acquired knowledge at every opportunity—use the techniques in this book whenever possible.

Principle No. 15 — The Health Principle

This book contains just about all there is to know about the subject of memory improvement. If you follow these principles and techniques, and if you creatively seek ways of implementing them, you will develop a memory that is far superior to what you had previously.

Yet, to be truly wise is to be aware of one's limitations. Memory, in the final analysis, is the result of the complex interactions of brain cells, and there is no way of getting inside one's skull to make the brain tissue perform better.

The amount of oxygen reaching the brain has been found to be a factor in brain performance. Elderly people who had failing memories were given large amounts of oxygen. While breathing the high percentage of oxygen, their ability to remember improved, according to recordings. Furthermore, the experiences learned while under the influence of oxygen were retained long afterward. Inasmuch as oxygen is carried by the blood, it would stand to reason that poor body circulation will deliver an inadequate supply of oxygen to the brain, hence inadequate mental performance. The human circulatory system will be affected by one's eating and drinking habits, and above all, by one's physical fitness. Exercise has been shown, of course, to aid physical well-being. Furthermore, exercise increases circulatory activity, causing the blood passageways to expand and permit freer traffic to all areas of the body, including the brain. Good health enhances mental functioning.

This section illustrated how a number of factors can work to aid memory and concentration. You can conclude that memory does not come about by magic. There are always one or more factors determining whether or not something will be remembered.

Keep in mind that the presence or use of any one of these mental factors and principles does not guarantee successful recall. We are speaking merely of tendencies. At any given time, the use of these principles and techniques will increase the *chances* of recall.

One concept prevails throughout this book—in order to commit information effectively to memory, *your mind must do something.* There is no way to get inside brains and turn a few secret switches and then produce a superb memory. You may visualize, associate, organize, discriminate, vocalize, think about information, find a use, become personally involved, set goals, review, or whatever—but you must do something. You must make an investment of mental energy. A number of suggestions for improving learning and memory have been and will be presented. It would certainly be impossible to apply all the principles at any one time. The techniques you use will depend upon your expectations of the future need for the knowledge. They depend, as well, on the structure and level of difficulty of the material. Whatever the circumstances, the learner cannot expect to let his/her brain lie back passively and absorb information. The fantasy of learning by playing a tape recorder while sleeping will never work. Optimum learning is a creative act. When incoming information is handled properly, it is selected, organized, interpreted, understood, and related. The product located in memory is often a better, more meaningful, and useful product than it was before the process.

All of the suggestions certainly cannot be applied in any one instance. In any situation, how does one decide which techniques shall be used, and to what degree? Frankly, there are no easy answers. The objective of the next chapter is to focus on typical situations and show how the principles apply to daily life.

part II

applying the basic principles

CHAPTER 5

how to remember names and faces

You are probably aware of the great psychological lift it gives to remember a person's name after only one meeting. Unfortunately, you are also probably aware of the frustration and embarrassment of forgetting. For many, the ability to remember names can be both economically as well as socially advantageous. You should apply the techniques given in this chapter at every opportunity.

Give full concentration

You must be convinced that it is important to remember a person's name as you are introduced. The most important step is to give your full attention to the introduction. Often a name is introduced and, two minutes later, you realize it is forgotten. Perhaps the reason was that, when you were being introduced, you were so busy thinking of the conversation that you never actually learned the name. As little as two minutes later, no technique of recall could possibly help. So, before you can do anything, you must give your *full* attention to the introduction.

When giving your full attention, do not be afraid to reveal that the person's name is important to you. If the person is introducing him/herself, watch intently. Get a clear visual picture of the way the lips move as the word is formed. Get a very clear picture of the face. Later on, in recall, if you are unsure of your memory of the face, you will probably forget the name that goes with it. On the other hand, gaining a full visual picture at the moment of introduction will give you an extra path to recall. You can often recall a name by referring to your visual image surrounding the introduction. If the person's expression, posture, clothes or anything else are recalled, the name will sometimes follow.

Review shortly after learning

The mind does most of its forgetting very shortly after learning. This factor is discussed further in the chapter on retention. If you do not use or think of the name as it would appear written the first minute or so following the introduction, you will most likely forget. The implication here is quite obvious. You must *review* a name shortly after you first hear it. While that person is speaking, you can quickly repeat the name to yourself. Or, better still, you should keep alert to the opportunity of using the name in an ensuing conversation. The person's name can be easily added to direct statements and questions. By simply getting into the habit of saying, "How do you do, Mr. Jones?", you will increase your retention enormously.

Look for outstanding features

Next, you must utilize the principle of discrimination. One of New York's foremost artists once told me of her dissatisfaction with her ability to remember faces. Very often she would briefly encounter people at art galleries and meetings. She was not concerned with remembering names necessarily, but with simply being able to recognize a person so as not to be offensive by not saying "Hello." I suggested that when she meets someone, she imagine what a caricature of that person would look like. (In a caricature drawing, the artist selects a facial feature that seems to stand out or characterize the person, and exaggerates it. To do so entails the process of discrimination.) This procedure worked for the artist and it will help anyone, whether they are artistic or not, to recognize faces.

When a person is introduced, you are often supplied with both the first and last names. Because the mind subconsciously senses difficulty in remembering this mass of unrelated information, the tendency is to turn off altogether. Yet rarely, if ever, would you have an immediate need to remember both names. Either the first or second is more important, depending upon the social situation. Just making the mental selection helps you remember not only the name you choose, but the other name as well, because the mind is more alert.

Recognize and create associations

Just getting into the habit of concentrating, discriminating, and using the name shortly afterward, will probably solve the severe problem of remembering names and faces. However, the object now is to convey methods that will make you an expert. You can develop the skill that will enable you to meet more than 20 people in a single evening and remember all their names.

If people were named Shorty, Skinny, Blue Eyes, etc., and they really did have those characteristics, you would have no difficulty remembering names because something about the person's physical appearance would remind you of the name. Similarly, if people were named Carpenter, Stupid, or Energetic, you would also perceive relationships as long as you knew something about the person. Of course, these convenient relationships are rarely encountered in everyday life. But if you are alert for relationships, they will pop up surprisingly often. You will see some five-foot-three-inch-tall man named Little or a man who loves to hunt named Hunter, or a woman with an extremely red face named Burns. Once you see these relationships, the technique is easy. You simply verbalize the relationship to yourself in the form of a sentence, such as "Mrs. Burns is so named because she has such a red and burnt face," and your eyes simultaneously focus on the uniqueness of her red face. Later, her red face will remind you of her name.

These relationships rarely exist, though. A person named Burns will usually have a normal complexion. Mr. Caine may not walk with a cane, and Mr. Green will certainly not look green. In these far more common situations where no relationship actually exists, why not create a relationship? Just unleash your imagination. If Mr. Green is not colored green, you may solve the problem by looking at him and making him green. Get a clear picture of the man in your mind and imagine him with a very green face. Upon seeing his face later, you will be reminded of the word "green" because his face and the color will become associated in your mind.

This, of course, is easier said than done. It takes practice—and when you practice you must make sure you really concentrate on performing the mental operations. On the opposite page there are eight people. Focus your eyes intently on number one. His name is Mr. Blue—make him blue. Now for number two—his name is Mr. Plum. He's holding a big plum. Number three is Ms. Grimes. She looks very grimy, indeed. Number four is Mr. Berger—make his head look like an iceberg. Number five is Ms. Carr—see her driving a car. Number six is Mr. Stone—his face is so hard looking, it is almost like a stone. Number seven is Ms. Byrd—you may have to go through some real mental contortions for this one, but you can do it. Number eight is Mr. Ax—the more vivid the better. Can you picture his head being chopped off by an ax? If you can, you won't forget his name.

Now, test your recall. Turn to page 41 and you will see these faces in scrambled order. Focus your attention on each one. Relax, and see if the associations will come back to you. If they do not, don't feel discouraged. It takes confidence and practice.

You may be aware of a minor problem. You may feel that this technique works fine for names such as Farmer, Hunter, Katz, Belz, and hundreds more, but these names are still not a majority. What about the majority of names that are not single syllables? What about those names that do not comprise a concrete word that you can visualize? For these, you select cues. A cue is something easily associated and remembered, and when recalled, will serve to remind you of the complete name. As an example, "Pen" will be a cue for the name Penfield. If you can look at the person and be reminded of a pen, this will in turn remind you of the name Penfield. If recall does not occur instantly, you can mentally transport yourself back to the moment when you were introduced. You picture yourself saying, "How do you do, Mr. Pen . . . Pen . . ?" and then the name Penfield will be retrieved.

The pitfall—mental inhibitions

As you may well imagine, all of your associations will not be flattering to the person whose name you wish to remember. In fact, many associations may be downright insulting. You must not let these matters interfere with your mental construction and creativity. No one has to know what is in your mind. I recall from my own experience a Mrs. Schwartz who was both amazed and flattered that I had remembered her name after a two-year interval. Of course, she had no way of knowing that I was aided greatly by my memory picture of a gigantic wart in the middle of her chin.

A suggestion: Make the association using the first connection that comes to your mind. This is a book on memory, not how to make friends.

SIMON LA GREE   ALBERT EINSTIEN   FAY WRAY

1.   NAPOLEAN BONAPART 2.   MARY SAD EYES   3.

4.   5.

6.   7.   8.

DUDLEY DO RIGHT   MRS LA GREE   ~~INSPECTOR~~ JUDGE
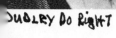 JONES.

During introductions, you must not look at a person for 10 seconds—and then suddenly burst out laughing.

Can you remember the cue but not the name?

In other words, is it possible that I could have suddenly blurted out, "Oh hi, Mrs. Wart." Or if the man is named Kelly for you to say, "Hello, Mr. Belly."

Although these errors in translation may occur occasionally, worrying about when they might happen causes more problems than it is worth. I remember one young woman returning to my class, and, not recalling her name immediately, I looked for an association. My eyes focused on her smooth, "creamy" face and "cream" came to my mind. But I stopped myself. "What kind of name is 'cream'?" I asked myself. So, applying recall technique (discussed in Part III) I threw out related names to myself. "Krame, Kramer, Crane, Kreen." I said to myself, "Kreen—that's it." "Hello, Mrs. Kreen," I said. But I was wrong. Her name was "cream" (spelled Kreme). You should not worry about errors in translation.

A quick method

In many instances, the following method for remembering names will be superior to the above. This method will work very well when you meet a large number of people at the same time.

This is initially a matter of discrimination. Pick something that you think stands out or is unique about the person. Select, preferably, a physical feature such as curly hair or big blue eyes. However, if nothing can be found, an article of clothing will do. In either case, connect your selection to the name and isolate the association. A few examples will help to illustrate the technique. You are introduced to a person who has very big blue eyes. The name is Blankenship. You isolate the blue eyes, and place them on a ship. (Notice that you do not include the face in your association.) You see another person wearing a bright blue tie. The name is Carney. So, you picture blue in a car. A person has a beard and the name is Gibson. You visualize a beard on the sun or on a famous person named Gibson.(This method works well for names that are hard to associate.) Later, when you see the person again and wish to recall the name, you ask yourself what object or feature you selected. Your selection will be retrieved with remarkable ease. You will then recall the name with information.

This method has some drawbacks, as you can see; no method is completely foolproof. If you use as your selection an article of clothing, recall will be difficult after a period of time because the person may be wearing different clothes. (Hardly an impossible situation, however—you can still remember by visually

transporting yourself back to a mental picture of the original introduction. If you can remember what the person was wearing, you can then remember your selection and recall that selection's association.) If you use a more permanent feature, such as a big nose or bushy eyebrows, interference may result, since many people have big noses and the same selections would be used over and over again.

On the other hand, this method is usually faster since you normally have time to select a feature many moments before the introduction and thus have half the connection ready.

Perhaps the best way to use this method is to take a quick moment to review. Reviewing can be accomplished by looking at each person and testing yourself to see if you can recall the selection you made, the association, and then the name. If the procedures were properly performed, ten names can be reviewed in about a minute or two. Also, bear in mind that if you use the name a few times, you may be able to discard the association.

Comparison of methods

Just in case there is any confusion as to the difference between Methods One and Two, here is an illustration, using the name "Geiger." With Method One, you might picture Mr. Geiger using a geiger counter. With Method Two, you would pick out some concrete feature of the person, and associate just that feature to a geiger counter. If he has blond hair, you would picture a **geiger** counter with blond hair. Although Method Two is normally used for meeting a large number of people at once, and Method One for normal situations, actually either method can be used depending upon your personal preferences.

Very often you can modify this method by treating your selection as part of a descriptive process. In actuality you would be combining both methods. As an easy example, say you selected curly hair as the outstanding feature, and you are told the name is Pat. You would picture yourself (note the principle of ego involvement) patting the hair. If the name were Gunther you would picture yourself shooting him in the feature you selected. You can make anything that the name describes happen to the feature.

Remembering first names

First names can be recalled by using either Method One or Method Two. Because most first names occur often, however, you can utilize still another method to connect a name and a face.

Upon hearing someone introduced as Bob you can immediately think of the first "Bob" that comes to your mind. You then notice just how much of the "new Bob" resembles the "other Bob." You can always find some feature that is common to both.

Just the act of searching the face and selecting the common feature will help your remember. If there is truly not an ounce of resemblance, you can verbalize the opposite relationship to yourself, and opposite associations are quite effective. Later on, in recall, you look at the man and you will notice just how much he resembles (or occasionally how much he does not resemble) the man you know named Bob, and that will be your trigger for recall.

Be sure to recall first names in this way—it works!

To remember a long sequence of names

"The technique of recognizing and forming associations works well," the almost-convinced reader may think, "but what happens when you are introduced to a large number of people in rapid succession?"

Picture a meeting with the chairperson introducing eight people. He/she says, "This is Mr. Hillary," and with hardly a second's pause between each introduction, "this is Ms. Gardner, Ms. Franklin, Mr. Ackerman, Mr. Kirkland," and so on. You barely have time to extend a handshake, nod, or make some other form of greeting, and certainly little or no chance to form associations. Actually, you can find relationships, "real" or "artificial," even under these circumstances, as long as you have plenty of creativity, confidence, and a lot of practice. It must be admitted, though, that for the average beginner, this method of introducing people can inundate by the barrage of data.

Do not let your progress be stalled by these circumstances. Bear in mind that your initial and most important objective in learning how to remember names is to be able to remember single names. If you can reach the level of proficiency where you are consistently able to remember one name every five minutes or so, while functioning normally during the intervening moments, your study and practice will be well rewarded.

As for the instances in which many names are introduced in rapid sequence, you must first understand that in these situations you are not really expected to remember the people's names. The introductions are done merely as a formality. Some may call it a matter of courtesy. If you do remember the names under such adverse conditions, realize that you are a bit of a performer.

Now that the problem of a long sequence of names may be seen in its proper place, here is a simple technique that will work wonders. Some people who will find this technique useful are salespeople, demonstrators, and anyone who participates in meetings, roundtables, or classroom discussions with new acquaintances.

The trick is easy and very effective once you note that, in most instances, people are located in a particular seat and they keep that seat throughout the dinner or meeting. Thus, you do not have to associate the name with the face, but merely the particular position. For example, suppose the eight people mentioned earlier are seated around a table and the chairperson, starting from left to right, introduces Mr. Hillary first. Immediately, you envision *yourself* on a hill. Ms. Gardner is next, and you see a garden on top of the hill. When Ms. Franklin is introduced, you may imagine Benjamin Franklin flying his kite in that garden, and so on for the remaining five.

At this point, you have in your memory storage all the material you need to recall the names of the individuals around the table. To remember the third person, you go through the chain and stop at the third association. Needless to say, though, this method is truly a trick. If you met the person the next day, or in fact anywhere other than in his/her original position, you would be in trouble. Therefore, you must build upon the original associations as soon as you have the chance.

Nevertheless you can still remember the name even when the positions no longer exist. You can refer to your original story chain, and you may recognize the correct name as you go through each association. Or, you may remember that the person was third in your story chain, and you would know it was the third association.

Remembering a small group

You are probably very often introduced to between two to four people. This may be the area which causes the most problems. This number is more difficult to remember than a single name, yet you are still expected to remember.

If you do not have the time to associate individually, then form a quick connection between each name. Occasionally, you may recognize a connection, if you are alert to it. You may be introduced to couples with names like Jack and Jill or Ronnie and Bonnie. If no easy connection exists, you can combine the names to form a single nonsense word. "Cliff" and "Karen" make Clifaren, or "Claren." For Beatrice, Tara, and Jack, you could construct Betarack. Bear in mind that you will have these names in your memory. All you will need is a little hint to get it out of storage.

Practice exercise

Thumb through a magazine, and for every face, associate the name that appears below. Go through the entire magazine. Then return to the beginning and test yourself. You should improve in speed and accuracy as you become more accustomed to the association techniques.

memory for facts

In this chapter, you will learn a basic method for remembering *anything*. Starting with the simplest fact—a word and its meaning—you will progress to learn how a large body of information can be committed to memory.

To commit a fact to memory, you must connect what we shall call a subject with information about that subject. If you want to connect a word and its meaning, the word is the subject, and the meaning is the information. To remember a book and its publisher, the title is the subject and the publisher is the information.

Often there is no natural connection between a subject and its information. You must learn how to bridge the gap.

Your mind must deal with smaller or more easily manageable units of information. The word "lambent" for example is more difficult to deal with mentally than a selected portion of the word; "lamb," is smaller, more familiar, and easily visualized. "Lambent" means bright, lively, radiant. Select the word "lamb" and now, dealing only with the smaller, more concrete unit, visualize that lamb and make it bright, lively, and radiant.

Later on, when faced with the word, you would trigger the recall process by first asking yourself what you selected. *Your selections will be recalled with remarkable consistency.* The rest is easy. You would think of, or visualize, only the selection, and in this case the visions of brightness and radiance would remind you of the meaning of the full word.

The same basic technique was mentioned in the previous chapter, when you learned a second method of associating names. If the individual has a very long nose, don't deal with the entire person. Deal with the smaller unit. If the information that goes with the subject is the name Lindsey, place that nose on a familiar face with that name.

Learning new words and isolated facts

"Acrimonious" means a sharp, biting remark. Visualize a rim that is so sharp, you know you would cut your mouth on it. Bring your emotions into it by thinking how awful that would be.

Sometimes you can form a visual association by changing the word slightly to form something concrete and familiar. "Libre" means "book" in French. See a slice of liver and place it in a book as a marker. Absurd? Perhaps, but remember one small point when forming mnemonic associations: the presence or absence of logic is not a factor in memory. It's not that logic should be avoided —but you must not waste time looking for a logical relationship if one is not readily apparent.

Take a few facts: You want to remember that the book *In Search of the Truth* was written by Ruth Montgomery. The title would be your subject. Select the word "Truth" and get it together with Ruth Montgomery. Later on, if someone were to ask you for the name of the author of *In Search of the Truth*, you would immediately recognize your selection. That would connect to "Ruth" which would remind you of "Montgomery." Sometimes you may have to select a cue for the information as well as the subject.

To remember that the date of the Spanish Inter-cultural Day is set for October 28, you would just change the subject into, perhaps, a fiesta. It will be difficult, however, to remember something as abstract as a date. Actually, any date can be converted into something more meaningful if you relate it to a holiday or event. In other words, you are much more likely to remember "three days before Halloween," than you are to remember "October 28." I'm sure you could now complete your picture. Notice that in this instance an extra step is involved. The pumpkin, or whatever you choose, must remind you of Halloween. This is not a problem, however. The number of stones you step on is not the crucial factor in whether you will be able to cross the river. It is the distance between each stone that matters.

Backward associations

Often you may have a need to recall the association in reverse. You may be asked what book Ruth Montgomery wrote. This is called a *backward association* and it is somewhat more difficult, whether or not memory techniques were used to learn the fact.

You would use the same recall procedure except that you must think of, or visualize, the information in recall, rather than the subject.

We all think differently. When you attempt to find specific cues, or ways of associating these cues, you will differ from others in your choices. This is acceptable and expected as long as your associations are clear and visual, and include all the desired facts.

Any fact or group of facts can be memorized through association. A drug salesman who wishes to remember the ingredients of his products should compose separate associations for each one. Empirin ™, for example, contains caffeine and aspirin. So he pictures himself standing next to the Empire State Building (cue for Empirin ™) while drinking coffee, which makes him wide awake (cue for caffeine), so he takes an aspirin. Later, when asked the ingredients for Empirin ™, he recalls them easily by picturing the Empire State Building.

Memory for foreign and technical vocabulary

You have already seen how association can aid the learning and recall of foreign words. Associations will not work for the learning of grammar and some other fine points of a language, but they will at least enable you to communicate the essentials. If you can recall nouns and verbs, you will at least have enough at your disposal to *use* the language in a foreign country. If you can just remember the words for "hotel," "street," "food," etc., you at least know you will survive—and as has been stated earlier, usage is the surest aid to retention.

By this time, the intelligent reader will realize that studying words by constructing artificial associations alone, will not be beneficial. He/she still needs a reasonably good knowledge of the word. The association is to be used strictly as a hint, a tiny but helpful shove in the right direction when normal memory fails. Mnemonics are of immense value, but the student must know their proper place.

In studying vocabulary correctly, whether the words be of a foreign language, or medical, legal, or scientific terms, the procedure is to learn the full meaning and correct usage first, and then associate.

The principle of organization can also play a part in the learning of new words, particularly for the student.

So often students of law, the biological sciences and English vocabulary have opportunities to see organization in the words they are studying, but instead treat each word as if it were assigned a meaning arbitrarily. That some words have organization can be shown by examining the word "psychopathology." Psych, path, and logy are root words meaning "mind," "disease" and "study," respectively. Therefore, you can easily see *why* "psycho-pathology" means the study of the diseases of the mind. The high school or college student should know the meanings of the most common Greek- and Latin-root words.

A common misinterpretation is the belief that by learning root words, one can "figure out" new words. If you carry this optimistic notion into the College Entrance Examination Boards, you will surely be disappointed. For instance, the root "cycl," means circle. If the student reads the sentence, "The stock market prices have been cyclic this decade," he/she will miss the point by assuming that prices have gone in circles. The structure of the words must be determined while you are studying. By learning how words are derived, you see that the words were not assigned meanings arbitrarily, and you gain an insight into their structure. The student should use the root words to learn *why* a word has a particular meaning. It is then that memory is strengthened.

The principle of ego involvement will often enhance memory and personal motivation in the learning of new words. The usual way that students approach the problem is to first look at the word, then the meaning, and repeat the association a few times. Most do not even bother to read the sentence which is provided to help the student gain a better understanding of the word's usage. Actually, the best way to approach the learning of a new vocabulary word or term is to first read the sentence that utilizes that word. After you read the sentence, do not look at the meaning of the word, but instead try to *figure out* the meaning by analyzing the word in the context of the sentence. After you have arrived at an answer, see if you are correct. If you are, fine; if not, this is still much better than just looking at the word and then the meaning. In either case, you are bringing yourself into the picture, by having a personal stake in learning the answer.

You can also become more involved by thinking of examples in which you personally become associated with the word. "Rationalize," for example, means using some logical reason to justify an improper act. All of us are guilty of this action at one time or another. To learn this word, think of the last time you found some reason for not doing a chore or assignment and describe it as a rationalization.

Relate isolated facts to a central theme

The mind absorbs information best when the new knowledge fits into structures and categories, as you saw in Part I. Barrage the mind with isolated facts, one not relating to the other, and it will escape into daydreams. You must not miss opportunities to tie information together.

Here is a brief look at some facts about Plato's philosophy: Plato set forth a great number of themes covering various aspects of the social sciences, among them his thoughts on education, the organization of the state, and who should be responsible for ruling the state. The average student would try to learn each of these separately. He would learn concepts as follows: (1) the state—to be so organized that it allows everyone to participate in a harmonious, moral, and just order; (2) purpose of education—to teach each person to be able to fit into his/her proper place in society; (3) ruling class—should be composed of the wisest men. When more information about Plato and other philosophers is added, it can become quite a chore to remember what each wrote about a particular topic.

All of the philosophers have a basic premise, an assumption underlying their principles about life, from which all their other ideas emanate. They arrive at their other ideas as an outgrowth of the basic underlying premise. It is necessary to find that premise and see how it relates to all their other ideas. Plato's basic premise, throughout all his writings, was his belief in a world of ideas where all things were perfect and unchanging for all time. This was the world of truth, goodness, and beauty. Complete knowledge of this world was unattainable for humans, but individuals differed in the amount of knowledge they possessed of the ideal world. Thus, the state should strive to become as close as possible to the "ideal" state, which was so organized that all its citizens could live a just and harmonious existence. The aim of education was to bring out the inherent wisdom, the ideal world within individuals, so that each could best participate in this just and moral order. The ruling class would be made up of those who had the most wisdom, the most knowledge of what was good, truthful, and just. These people had the closest approximation of the ideal world in their minds. These people's judgments would be based on the *ideal world* rather than the selfish instincts of the world known to the masses.

In this way you can see the facts of Plato's philosophy as related to the major idea. You can see "sense" in your material. You are not remembering a bunch of isolated facts. As a result of studying and learning by seeing organization, you acquire more knowledge and retain that knowledge with less effort. In remembering, you may not always be able to recall immediately what Plato's ideas were on education, but by first referring to his basic premise, the minor themes soon return.

Classification and association can work together

Very often you can associate a fact not with a name, place, object, or idea, but rather with a position. This position in turn will provide information. Here is an example: A marketing manager in the advertising field was dealing with dozens of accounts. Each company had an advertising manager, a product manager, a sales promotion manager, an artist, and a copywriter, and he had to deal with all of them. He was constantly confusing the advertising manager of Avon with the sales promotion manager of Squibb or with the product manager at Bendix, and so on. He kept neat notes, but at times that method proved to be a time-consuming and embarrassing procedure. I showed him how, if asked who is the copywriter at Bendix, for example, he could immediately draw from his mental file of hundreds of people, positions, and companies, and come up with the right name.

His first step was to categorize his material. Instead of aimlessly trying to remember a name, and associating it with that man's position and company, he started with the company name and committed each position, in turn, to memory. He progressed in a set order. He remembered first the advertising manager, then the sales promotion manager, then the product manager, next the copywriter, and last the artist. (The reason for that particular order will be explained shortly.) Each company was treated as a separate category and that mental action alone aided memory.

The next step was to select cues for each company and associate each person's name in the order designated by their company positions. Take the first company, Pepsi-Cola, and select a cue. You might visualize a bottle of Pepsi ™. Let us say the advertising manager is Baron. (The Pepsi ™ is being drunk by a baron.) The sales promotion manager is Parkinson. (Drinking Pepsi ™ takes place in a park.) The product manager is Wendt. (It gets windy. Remember, all that is needed is a cue. Windy will remind one of Wendt if the individual has had any prior dealing with the name.) Manchester is the copywriter. (Wind blows against the baron's chest.) The artist is Crowley. (Put a crow into the story somehow.) Please review this chain for the recall test that is coming.

The next step is not actually a step but rather a realization of the fact that you do not have to remember each person with their job title. All you have to do is remember the name and note its *position* along the chain and that will tell you the job title. For example, if you want to know the product manager of Pepsi-Cola, you would visualize the Pepsi ™ bottle, see the visions being recalled, and note that wind is the third association. You would then know that the name resembling wind would be the product manager of Pepsi ™. Why? Because you kept the same order of job titles for all the companies. The product manager of the company is always the third association.

The last step is not totally necessary if you are actually using a system like this in your job situation. Familiarity itself will enable you to recall the order of job titles effortlessly after a while. Nevertheless, at the beginning it is necessary to establish an aid to remembering the order of the job titles. Otherwise, the marketing manager, in this example, could remember that Wendt is the third association connected to Pepsi-Cola but forget who the third association represented. Thus a cross-association was used, utilizing a simple letter chain. A for Advertising Manager, S for Sales

Promotion Manager, P for Product Manager and so on until the letter chain ASPCA was formed. Hence the reason for that particular order of job titles.

Try one more company on your own, using your own cues and story chain. Note that since you are now using an entirely different story chain, you cannot possibly get the names in one company mixed up with the names of another. That is the beauty of this method. Practice, concentrate, review, and afterward you will test your knowledge of Pepsi-Cola and this next company, which is Avon.

Choose your cue for Avon. Following are the personnel:

Advertising Manager — Preston
Sales Promotion Manager — Kramer
Product Manager — Byrd
Copywriter — Servatius
Artist — Purton

Make up a truly wild, no-holds-barred story.

Without looking back, see if you can answer these questions:

1. Who is the Product Manager of Pepsi-Cola?
2. Who is the Sales Promotion Manager of Avon?
3. Who is the Copywriter of Pepsi?
4. Who is the Advertising Manager of Avon?
5. What position does Servatius hold at Avon?
6. What position does Manchester hold at Pepsi?

If you did commit the chains to memory and tested yourself, I am sure you can see the enormous potential in using a system such as this. Any number of companies, positions, and names could be mentally filed in this manner.

The applications of this technique are enormous. Categorizing and associating can be extended to a great variety of material, particularly in the area of scholastics. Taking a course in philosophy, for example, a student will read works or summaries of a number of philosophers and be expected to know what each one said. Trouble in reading can be encountered, however, because they all set forth a great number of ideas concerning various aspects of the social sciences, and they do so in no common order. Reading with no particular purposes will scramble your brain. Yet you can organize the material and your objectives once you recognize that all of the philosophers (or psychologists, economists, or whatever) touch upon the *same issues or topics.* They all eventually discuss how the state or country should be organized. They all discuss who should be responsible for governing. They all give their views on the purpose of education, and so on. Recognizing this, you should form a list of topics. Set up the topics in order, and, for each philosopher, construct a story chain with cues for each topic. Your ultimate objective is to write under each topic first what Plato said about it, then Aristotle, and so on down the line. As each philosopher is studied in turn, the student should seek purposes and comparisons for each topic in order. This technique will dramatically improve efficiency, and change a dull, aimless activity into something purposeful and enjoyable.

Visual chains for you?

You may be thinking that visual associations are great for those rare, super minds who can construct and remember them, but that you are not one of those gifted few. This is a natural reaction to the discomfort encountered in trying something new and different. Although individuals do vary in their ability to create and visualize associations, the chances are that you possess more proficiency in these techniques than you realize.

You should do more about mnemonics and visual chains than simply nod in agreement that they can be useful. Frankly, there is nothing to be said that will convince you. Only you can prove their value, and you do that by usage.

Anyone in business or professional life can probably find many ways to utilize the principle of association. The real skill is in being creative, in finding methods of utilizing the technique for your own unique situation.

Visualization, association, and the reduction of stress

There may be an added benefit in converting information from the complex and abstract to concrete and familiar visions, and then chaining the visions together in a story. At this point in the history of research in psychology, there can be no doubt that stress plays an important role, not only in personality but in health. The mind affects the body.

It is my belief that the manner in which we deal with information can add to or detract from the amount of stress we incur. I became interested in this subject when I asked a businessman friend what he did to relax after his hard day. He replied that playing chess was his most relaxing activity. That was understandable. In this modern age, the need for abstractions has forced us to deal with words and the verbal area of the brain far more than the visual area. We remember words, talk with words, think with words. This overloading of activity may be a source of tension. Whenever the mind works in visual terms there seems to be a balancing and consequently relaxing effect. This is probably the reason for the increasing popularity of meditation, which is nothing more than extended, intense, visual imagery. Some suspect that even our daydreams are helpful, and that at least some daydreaming is desirable psychologically. Certainly our nightly dreams have value too. If an individual is consistently awakened as soon as dreaming starts, he/she quickly develops the same behavioral symptoms that indicate severe tension.

It appears that any diversion of mental activity from the verbal area to the visual will be beneficial. Certainly there are many instances in which you can visualize, if you are alert to them. How often have you started out to get a list of groceries and repeated the items to yourself? You could just as easily visualize the items for the same length of time, or visualize yourself selecting the items from the shelves. In so doing you would be taking some of the burden off the verbal area. The same is true in the use of visual associations. You are taking information that would surely go to the verbal area. By selecting something concrete and easily visualized about the information, and then connecting your selection to the desired knowledge, you are transferring the mental activity from one area to another.

Can the visual area eventually be overused as is the verbal? It does not seem so. It seems that we have boundless capacities for imagining. Visualizing is not as subject as verbalizing is to the interference factor (discussed in Chapter 12). As long as you do not confine your imagination to what is normal or logical, you can make great use of visual associations.

CHAPTER 7

how to read for concentration and retention

One of the characteristics of the mind is that it thrives on what is best described as *meaning*. A couple of examples here illustrate the term. Sometimes, we hear words, words, and more words, but nothing sinks in. Suddenly, we get the idea. The material takes on meaning and we absorb. For instance: the word "a" and "red" taken together do not hold any meaning as far as the brain is concerned. Add the word "apple" and you have a phrase that the brain can deal with. "A red apple" has meaning.

A second characteristic of the mind is that it seems to thrive on activity during our non-sleeping hours. In fact, it is impossible to keep the mind completely inactive and blank for any length of time. The one thing that is probably more difficult than keeping the mind fixed on a train of thought is to have it go blank altogether. We must always be thinking about something. This next section shows how the two principles of meaning and activity can affect concentration while reading.

Improve your reading habits

Undoubtedly you have encountered the phenomenon of reading a page, getting about halfway down, and suddenly realizing that your mind has been way out in left field. This is usually due to poor reading habits. True justice to this topic can only be accomplished by thorough instruction and practice in the principles of developmental reading. Following is a discussion of the basic principle as it applies to concentration.

Basically, the problem is that when reading poorly, one word at a time and repeating each word silently, the average reader takes in printed symbols at such a slow rate that the brain becomes distracted. If the reader comes to the phrase "the red apple," he/she first focuses on the word "the" and repeats the word to him/herself. Unfortunately, "the" by itself doesn't mean anything as far as the brain is concerned. Next, he/she focuses on "red" and repeats that word. Still no information has been transmitted to the brain and "red" by itself means nothing until the word "house," "barn," or another noun is added. The reader cannot expect his/her brain to just lie in a blank state and wait for information to be fed to it. If input information is fed too slowly, the brain will generate activity on its own. It is understandable that an intelligent and active mind will wander at this point. The good reader, on the other hand, takes in the entire phrase in one glance, and instead of hearing the words in his/her head, the only thing that enters his/her mind is the image of the fruit that these words represent. Admittedly, breaking the habit of reading one word at a time, and subvocalizing (repeating the words silently to one's self) isn't easy, but when effective reading skill is attained, both reading speed and concentration are immensely improved.

Reading faster for concentration

The following is a phrase that is upside down. Focus your eyes on the middle of the words and try to see the entire group with only one glance.

ʎɐʍ ʎɯ ƃuᴉoƃ

Perhaps you found that easy. Now try the same phrase right side up.

going my way

Most likely that was more difficult. Unless you are a skilled reader, your eyes had an inclination to jump from one word to the next. Yet, the fact that your eyes were able to effortlessly take in the first phrase, shows that the eyes are easily able to take in a span which comprises more than one word. The only reason you found the second exercise difficult is because of bad reading habits which are characteristic of the overwhelming majority of people. These habits can be broken with practice.

When people have difficulty in keeping their mind on the material, they often read slower, subvocalizing every "it," "the," and "to." Comprehension will suffer because the reader is forced to give some of his/her attention to the physical act of speaking. Generally, reading slower does not help concentration. Instead, try reading faster, in groups of words.

It may be objected that reading faster will reduce comprehension. In many cases, this is true. However, without exception, one attains greater comprehension on successive readings. Usually one understands and retains more by reading a chapter two or three times rapidly, than once slowly.

Adjust reading rate

This is not to say that in all instances you should increase reading speed. Actually, the speed of reading should depend upon the level of difficulty of the material. You can read light fiction perhaps five times as fast as a technical article in a professional journal. Yet, in every article there is a considerable amount of easy reading, and you must adjust your reading rate as you go along.

One problem most people have that causes lapses of concentration in reading, is that they make no effort to adjust their reading rate to fit the material. Almost invariably they are on the slow side, reading easy passages at the same rate as difficult ones. In essence, the objective is to supply input information to the brain at a rate that the brain can deal with. Faster than this optimum level causes a loss in comprehension. Slower than this level causes mind-wandering.

To increase speed, you could try to reduce subvocalization. Of course, this is easier said than done, and normally it requires a full course in speed reading to accomplish that one objective. Nevertheless you can practice it on your own. You may ask, "If I do not say the words to myself as I read, then what does my mind do while reading? What do I think about?" These are darn good questions. The answer is that the mind has plenty to keep it occupied. You may also fear that there is a loss in retention when you stop repeating words to yourself. After all, repetition is a common technique for remembering. When you wish to remember shopping items or directions, you often repeat the information a few times, and that enhances memory. In this chapter you will see how to replace subvocalization with other forms of mental activity. In so doing, you will read faster, comprehend and remember more, and, above all, improve concentration.

Visualize

If, as you go along, you are recording a story or instructions in your imagination, your mind will not wander. Visualization is discussed in many areas in this book, and it is particularly effective as a reading technique. Practice by reading light, easily visualized fiction. Your improved concentration will carry into other areas.

Photographic memory

You probably occasionally hear people speak wistfully of a photographic memory. With a photographic mind, supposedly one can reproduce every detail of a page in picture form, every number, every letter, even mustard stains. Photographic memory does not exist. There is no one who can memorize a page with an efficiency even remotely comparable to a camera. Numerous interrogations of people claiming such an ability have revealed that their memory is not photographic. The page is not recalled in its original form, but rather it is distorted, invariably made larger, by the imagination. Furthermore, unimportant details are not "photographed."

Nevertheless, these people do have a remarkable ability to remember. What they actually do is utilize the same visual capacities which you have been learning about and developing. The only real difference is that the "photographic" method visualizes the actual written word, or attempts to visualize the actual written information, while the usual method visualizes what the information describes. You should employ both methods. Graphs and illustrations can often be visualized without distortion by "photographic" imagery. Photographic memory may not be what it is cracked up to be, but reproducing written information is possible, and the skill can be improved with practice.

I remember taking a multiple choice test for a course in mental retardation. One question stumped me. The question dealt with the approach a certain organization took in classifying the mentally retarded. One of the four choices was "a developmental approach." I first visualized the textbook and then I tried to remember where on a page I had seen the name of the organization. I was able to recall a reasonably certain picture of the name being at the top of a page, on the left hand side of the book. The image was still far too cloudy to serve as recall for the definition itself. My "photograph" did contain, however, a subtitle, at about the middle of the page, which was about a man named Piaget, a developmental psychologist. From there, the next step was to make an "educated guess," that the "developmental" approach was probably correct, judging from the author's construction of ideas. I learned later that I was correct.

This method of recall is hardly superhuman. Anyone can recall in this way with practice. When reading, occasionally look up and try to recall the position on a page of key statements and subtitles. You will be surprised at your ability after a while.

Create an experience

Things are happening all of the time, but they are not experiences. When something happens to you, it becomes an experience. Our mind has a natural tendency to focus on things that affect us, and becomes quickly bored and subject to distractions if the information does not affect our lives. Therefore, one sure way to become personally involved is to convert material into personal experience. Whenever possible, create visions that place yourself in the story, situation or problem.

Imagining yourself as Napoleon or Lincoln or Churchill will foster increased concentration in history. You may learn about the customs and culture of another land by imagining how you would feel living in the country. If you are reading about the farm problem in economics, imagine you are the President of the United States, faced with the necessity of making a decision on price supports. Each idea presented to you from then on will have an effect on your decision, which you know must be arrived at by the end of the chapter.

Finding organization

Ordinary conversation has a definite structure of ideas, as you saw on page 21. In fact, there is organization almost any time anything is communicated. Yet, if you fail to perceive organization in your reading material, you are inviting the conditions of *mind-wandering* and *poor retention*.

Which figure, "A" or "B," is easier to reproduce from memory?

Fig. A   Fig. B

Figure "A," of course, is easier. "A" is organized into a distinctive, recognizable pattern.

Material is both easier to learn, as well as easier to recall, if it is organized. However, a large part of the process depends upon you and how you perceive your material. It is a two-way street. In the above, figure "A" is easier because you cannot help but notice the pattern. Figure "B" is tough for the mind to deal with, but if you look closely, you can find the organization. The first two long lines on the left have no little line between them. Between the first and fifth of the long lines (going from left to right), you can recognize the progression 0, 1, 2, 3 of short lines. It can also be seen that each of the smaller lines in each group increases in size. Now you can reproduce figure "B" easily. What have you done? The figure did not change in appearance. Rather, it is your own perception of the pattern that has changed. When you can perceive or recognize the relationships between things, you enhance memory. Sometimes, material is presented in a poor way, but the reader or listener is motivated enough to make sense out of the material, and it is then retained. At other times an author works to exhaustion to present the material in an organized manner, but the reader fails to pay heed to his/her efforts, and mind-wandering or poor comprehension results.

When information is communicated, it usually comes in an organized structure. Recognizing that structure improves comprehension, and furthermore, just looking for that structure while reading will improve concentration. Practice looking for organization in reading by starting with the paragraphs in the following reading exercises. It is important to realize that each paragraph contains only one idea. There may be many facts, descriptions, words, or examples, but only one idea.

Main idea exercises

Each paragraph contains a main idea. When an author has fully explained or elaborated upon one idea in one paragraph, he/she begins a new paragraph for the purpose of presenting the next main thought. In many informative or technical paragraphs the main idea is clearly stated in one sentence, usually the first one. Sentences stating main ideas are called "topic sentences," for they present the limited topic to be discussed. The remainder of the paragraph is a development and explanation of that topic.

The main idea of the following paragraph is made explicit in a topic sentence. Read this paragraph, then locate that sentence. Select, from choices a-d, the main idea as expressed by the sentence you located.

SAMPLE EXERCISE #1

The speed with which a child develops the ability to talk is dependent upon the amount of attention and stimulation he/she receives. For example, the child whose parent spends time identifying objects and simply talking to him/her, is likely to develop the ability to speak early. On the other hand, a child who grows up in an institution, or with a parent who pays him/her little attention, is likely to develop language facility at a slower rate.

The choice which expresses the main idea is:
a) The child whose parent plays and talks to him/her learns to speak early.
b) A child who is ignored by his/her parent learns to speak late.
c) The ability to talk depends on how much stimulation a child receives.
d) The speed with which a child develops his/her ability to talk depends on how much stimulation he/she receives.

The correct choice is d, for it expresses that idea about which the paragraph is written. Choices a and b relate facts stated in this paragraph, but they are not the idea that is the theme of the selection. Rather, they are two facts which help support the

59

main idea as expressed in d. Though the first sentence presents the main idea of this selection, there is no rule that the topic sentence may not appear elsewhere in any paragraph. At other times the main idea is not stated in any one sentence. In such cases the main idea is implied by the entire contents of the selection. Read the following paragraph, then select the main idea it implies.

SAMPLE EXERCISE #2

Divide the year into 12 months of four weeks each and add one day, which shall belong to no month but shall have a special name, such as New Year's Day. On leap years add an extra day, either following New Year's Day or, preferably, following some month in the summer, and give it some special name. Such a plan would allow the first, eighth, fifteenth, and twenty-second days of each month to be any day decided upon, say Sunday, and a single sheet would answer for all months and years. All holidays would fall on the same day of the week in each year, and if the ecclesiastical calendar were fixed so that Easter Sunday would fall on some particular Sunday, the entire problem would be greatly simplified.

The main idea of this paragraph is:
a) How to account for leap years.
b) How to fix a dateless New Year's Day.
c) How to simplify the calendar.
d) Holidays should fall on fixed days.

As you can see, the entire paragraph is a description of the simplified calendar. As such, it implies c as its main thought.

Read the paragraphs that follow, and select and record the main idea of each one. If you are unsure of the correct answer, simply ask yourself how you would transmit the message of the paragraph in as few words as possible.

READING EXERCISE #1

Several of the most primitive tribes of Australia and Africa use a number system which has neither 5, 10, nor 20 as a base. Most of these tribes employ a base 2, never using single numbers, but counting in pairs. So strong is this sense of pairing that a native will seldom notice if two shells have been removed from a row of seven, but he/she will immediately be aware if only one is missing. Perhaps the number base of these primitive tribes had its origin in dividing the food from the hunt into equal portions.

The main thought of the paragraph is that:
a) Many tribes don't use 5, 10, or 20 as a number base.
b) Many tribes count by pairing.
c) The sense of pairing in primitive tribes is stronger than their sense of numbers.

d) Counting was originated by hunters.

e) The base 10 system is the best for mathematical calculations.

READING EXERCISE #2

Charles Hogman was born with serious physical defects because his mother was stricken with German measles during the early stages of her pregnancy. Charles, now eighteen years old, sued his mother's physician in New Jersey on the grounds that the doctor had not advised his mother to abort him. In New York State, a child conceived as a result of rape in a New York mental institution sued the state. His grounds were that the state should have prevented his conception by mentally deficient, unmarried parents. In Illinois, an illegitimate child sued his father, claiming the father had placed him at a disadvantage by bringing him into existence as an illegitimate child. Although the courts denied all these claims, the existence of these lawsuits indicates a new sociological trend: people are beginning to value the quality of human life over the fact of mere existence.

The main thought of the paragraph is that:

a) Courts denied payment to all claims of "disadvantaged" births.

b) Many unplanned births occur.

c) Abortion laws are outdated and need revision.

d) The quality of human life is increasing.

e) None of the above.

READING EXERCISE #3

Man is unique in that he does not have to live only in the present. His world is extended by symbolic thought to include past history and future time. He can read about the extinct civilization of the Incas, and, using scientific knowledge, speculate as to the nature of the universe. Of course, no modern man has witnessed the Inca civilization or touched a star, yet he can talk about them knowingly because of symbols. The planet Pluto, in fact, was first discovered mathematically by scientists long before its existence was actually verified visually by means of high power telescopes.

The main thought of the paragraph is that:

a) Pluto was first discovered mathematically.

b) Man is unique.

c) Man lives in the past, present, and future.

d) Symbols extend man's existence.

e) None of the above.

READING EXERCISE #4

South America, as a whole, is a rich continent. It does not, however, have the geographical conditions which make for favorable economic development. High ranges of mountains prevent easy transportation within the continent itself. Most of the farmland is so inaccessible that the population must toil hard for a living. There is little iron or coal, and the climate in many regions is too hot to be conducive to sustained physical effort.

Which of the choices most closely restates the main thought?

a) South America is a rich continent.
b) Mountain ranges in South America interfere with transportation.
c) South America's climate is not favorable to economic development.
d) South America's geographic conditions are hostile to developing a modern, efficient economy.

READING EXERCISE #5

On May 14, 1607, when the first settlers arrived in Virginia, life was easy. But, within the short span of two months, conditions changed drastically for the worse. The Indians became cautious and distrustful, and provisions began to run low. Some food was spoiled, and, with the coming of the hot weather, the brackish drinking water became contaminated. In August, death struck often and quickly, taking, among others, Captain Gosnold. Inexperience, unwillingness, or inability to do the hard work that was necessary, and the lack of adequate information about how to survive in a primitive wilderness, led to bickering, disagreements, and inaction.

The main thought of the paragraph is that:

a) The first settlers faced many hardships when they arrived in Virginia.
b) Conditions for the early settlers deteriorated steadily.
c) After the first two months Indians became distrustful.
d) Conditions for the early settlers deteriorated steadily within the first two months.

ANSWERS

b, e, d, d, d.

Organization in chapters and articles

To communicate information, letters are organized to form words. Words are organized into sentences, and, as you have seen, sentences are organized into unified paragraphs of ideas. When information is communicated properly, the paragraphs also form a definite structure.

It is crucial in dealing with the problem of concentration that the reader be aware of the author's trend of thought (I am referring now to technical or semi-technical reading, not light fiction). As quickly as possible, you should attain a reasonably good idea of the path along which the author will lead you. If you let your mind just passively lie back, it will fly elsewhere when suddenly bombarded with information. This chapter will suggest ideas on how to recognize and perceive organization on the part of the author. It is a skill that gets better with practice. Therefore, it is wisest to read a wide range of material and become familiarized with different styles of presentation.

The editorial on page 77 illustrates the simple but effective pattern in which an author states a problem, and follows it with a list of causes, reasons, or suggestions.

Often organization can be determined by the textbook system of subtitles and headings. Starting below is the first page of a chapter from a well known, well organized, history textbook. You can see the name of the chapter and immediately assume that the purpose of the chapter is to describe what life was like in the antebellum period. The author has categorized the information into a number of headings or titles. Each heading describes one aspect of American life during the period. Each heading is cohesive. It may refer to, or draw upon, other categories. The general theme of the first heading is to describe the development of nationalism. You can see that confidence is given as a reason for the growth of nationalism. The paragraphs that follow tell why the people were confident. The mental act of taking note of this organization prepares the brain to receive related information and facilitates concentration.

When you look at one fact, in perspective, it can take on a much broader significance. You can remember simply that gold was discovered in 1850 or you can gain a better overall appreciation of the discovery and how it affected history. Gold was discovered, which increased prosperity, which gave people more confidence in the country, which in turn helped to cause nationalism, a characteristic of the antebellum period.

Because facts are tied together in this way, the entire structure is strengthened. Suppose you forget "nationalism." You can then try to recall certain facts. If you happen to remember gold being discovered, the chain can work in this reverse order to help you remember the creation of confidence and nationalism.

Life in the Antebellum Period

1   *Nationalism Unlimited*

Confident America · To most Americans in the early 1850's, it was wonderful just to be alive. The recent violent struggle over the Wilmot Proviso had, it is true, raised dark warnings of disruption of the Union and even war. But in the compromise measures of 1850 good sense and devotion to the Union had once again prevailed over sectionalism, just as they had triumphed during the crises over Missouri in 1819-1820 and Nullification in 1832-1833. Everywhere, in the South as much as in the North and West, men breathed loud sighs of relief when it seemed that all sections would accept the Compromise as the "final" settlement of the vexing issue of slavery in the territories. This was true especially after a hot fight over the Compromise in Georgia in 1851 resulted in a sweeping victory by the champions of the Union.

Of course there were dark clouds gathering just below the horizon. As we will soon see, Northerners were unwilling to accept one part of the Compromise, the Fugitive Slave Act. Southerners would not remain content with exclusion of slavery from any part of the territories. And pent-up tensions would erupt in secession and war at the beginning of the sixties. But this future was hidden or only dimly seen as Americans looked ahead in 1851.

The fifties were a decade of high and generally sustained prosperity, except for a setback in 1857. Gold from California swelled the money supply. The frontier was expanding at a rapid pace. Foreign trade was growing by leaps and bounds. To a people who had just carved out a western empire, fulfilled their "Manifest Destiny," and were busy growing great, no problem seemed too difficult to solve.

Expanding national pride and jaunty confidence were evident on all sides throughout the fifties, even during the middle and latter years of the decade, when sectional strife once again was menacing. Aggressive nationalism permeated the popular literature and the speeches of politicians. It took form especially in the new twist that public spokesmen in the late 1840's and the 1850's gave to the older doctrine of "Manifest Destiny." Before about 1848 Americans had conceived of their destiny in terms of expansion to the Pacific Coast. Now they were beginning to think in bolder terms—of a mission to show the world, particularly decadent Europe, the superiority of democratic institutions; of a destiny, perhaps, to govern the entire Western Hemisphere!

Aggressive Diplomacy · Such confidence was reflected most vividly during the fifties in the statements of men who spoke for the United States abroad. When democratic revolutions swept over Western Europe in 1848 our government was quick to express its sympathies for peoples struggling for freedom. In December, 1850, Secretary of State Daniel Webster sent a defiant message to the Austrian minister in Washington. The latter had complained of the sympathy that the United States had shown to Hungary in her struggle for independence. "The power of this Republic at the present moment," Webster boasted, "is spread over a region one of the richest and most fertile on the globe, and of an extent in comparison with which the possessions of the House of Hapsburg are but a patch on the earth's surface."

In the summer of 1853 Senator Douglas of Illinois made a trip abroad and probably expressed the sentiments of a large proportion of his fellow countrymen when he wrote: "Europe is tottering to the verge of dissolution." And Henry Clay, on his deathbed, wrote to the Hungarian patriot, General Louis Kossuth, that "for the cause of liberty we should keep our lamp burning brightly on this western shore, as a light to all nations."

Finding organization in material without subtitles

Chapters occasionally do not have a system of headings and subtitles. Some have headings but do not follow a coherent organization. This presents more difficulty. However, certain techniques can be employed. Reading the first and last paragraphs will often reveal the trend. Summaries at the end, if provided, should always be read first; this will make you aware of the main points as well as raise some questions in your mind. Also, much can be learned about the progression of thought by scanning for the main idea in each paragraph. Less often, the main idea will be stated in the last sentence. Still less often it will not be stated but implied. Nevertheless, approximately 80 percent of the time, a great deal of knowledge about the organization of the material can be gained by reading the first sentence and, if it is not then located, by jumping to the last.

Central ideas can often be located in scanning, by looking for key words or phrases such as: "therefore," "finally," "as a result of," etc. Central ideas often directly follow these words, and you can discover the author's pattern more quickly by stopping to read the sentences within which these key words are found.

To obtain a better idea of how to find organized thoughts in material without subtitles, suppose you had to read an article entitled, "Supreme Court Requires Radical Changes." You can approach this article in the following manner: Pretend you are giving a speech and your first statement is that the Supreme Court requires radical changes—what type of content has to follow shortly afterwards? Naturally, you have to give reasons. Then, after stating "why," would the author next state "how" the Supreme Court should be changed?

Discriminate

If you look for organization in reading material, it becomes obvious that ideas vary tremendously in value. That is as it should be. Statements may take up equal space on paper, but they must not take up equal space in your mind. Some statements should be skimmed, others should be read carefully, and still others should be reviewed and firmly committed to memory. It may be objected that this may seem like an invitation to carelessness. True carelessness, though, is spending time on non-essentials. That same time could have been used to organize, review, or give more attention to important ideas. Probably most mind-wandering stems from the act of plodding along, giving equal treatment to each word. If someone is reading with an intent to discriminate, signals unrelated to intention are expelled more quickly *while the mind is more sensitive to those few signals that do relate.* As a result, efficiency is enhanced.

Reading for a purpose

One sure way to employ the principle of discrimination is to use the technique of reading for a purpose. Have you ever noticed how some baseball players, while in their batting stance awaiting the pitcher's throw, will wave their bat slightly? Or that they repeatedly open and close their hands around the bat? Watch how great hitters hold their bat away from their bodies instead of letting it rest comfortably on their shoulders. These are not idiosyncratic, meaningless actions by the ballplayers. They all have the purpose of directing the brain's attention to the parts of the body that will soon be used, namely the hands and wrists. Holding the bat at a distance, or waving it, creates pressure on the hands. The nerves extending to and from the hands are alerted and primed for instantaneous action.

Neurons in the brain can also be alerted to receive information. By gaining an overview of the chapter as a consequence of scanning, you call certain cells to attention and prepare them to receive information. You call cells to attention when, after scanning, you state your purpose in reading. *Reading for a purpose is probably the single most important factor in concentration.*

Usually, reading with the author's organization in mind, and reading with an intent to seek those ideas that relate to the author's structure, will just naturally entail the act of reading for a purpose. Sometimes, however, you may be looking for other facts or ideas related to other objectives. Nevertheless, you must always consciously be looking for something. Just as a missile will be unable to stay on course unless it is programmed for an exact destination, so it is with the mind. Suppose you come to the sentence, "Banks act as clearinghouses for the exchange of money and credit for groups within the country." Any number of things may come to your mind. The sentence may serve to remind you to make a withdrawal from the bank because the car needs repair, which in turn causes reflection as to which service station to go to, which reminds you that the place on the corner did a lousy job last time, and so on. Or you may think of a clear, glass house, taking out a loan, and many, many more things. Any time you hear, feel, or see something, the signal may go off in any number of directions. But when you are reading with a definite purpose in mind, the signals reject all connections and pathways that have no bearing on your destination.

Concentration does not necessarily mean keeping your mind fixed on one object or in one place. When reading, it means keeping your thoughts moving toward a definite end. Note that when your purpose is sharply defined, you can cruise through material at an extremely rapid rate and your mind will not wander. If you are looking for someone's name in a phone book, your eyes can cruise down the page at a remarkable speed; or if you are looking up some specific information from an encyclopedia, such as a famous person's birthdate, you can proceed quite rapidly until you come to key words such as "born," or "birth," or to the date itself. And does your mind wander under such circumstances?

Of course, you normally do not wish to look for only one fact in a chapter, as that would mean excluding too much information. Nevertheless, all reading has a happy medium. The exact purposes in reading depend upon the contents of the chapter as well as the background and short-range goals of the reader.

A purpose is created when the reader wants to gain some particular knowledge or understanding from the reading which follows. The main idea of the following paragraphs should address the purpose. For example, setting a purpose to learn the size of a red blood cell would be too specific, answerable by a minor detail. On the other hand, setting out to find out what red blood cells are like would be too vague, comprising too many areas of subject matter. Intending to find out how red blood cells obtain food is an example of a happy medium.

A simple way to establish a purpose—ask questions

A good way to establish a purpose is to ask questions. Upon beginning any technical article, you should first look at its title, overall structure, and length. You might find a question simply in the title of the article. You might change the title "Functions of Living Cells" to the question "What Are the Functions of Living Cells?" If you do, your purpose in reading is to find ideas, facts, and principles that will enable you to answer the question which you have raised.

The title of an article is "Victims of a Curse." Upon noting the title, you would raise three questions immediately—What does the curse consist of? Who are the victims? and, Why are they cursed? On the other hand, the structure might suggest a question. For example, as in the above-mentioned article on living cells, you notice that the subtitles read "the cell membrane," "cytoplasm," and "nucleus." So your questions could be "What are the parts of a cell?" and "What are the functions of each part?"

READING EXERCISE #6

Set your purposes before reading the following article. Note the title. What purposes come to mind? Perhaps you will want to find out what the curse consists of. Who are the victims? You may also want to know if and how the curse affects us. Read *solely* for the purpose of finding the answers to these, or similarly stated questions. When you are finished, look up and construct a summary of the article around your purposes. In other words, you begin your summary by first stating what the curse consists of. If you state the ideas clearly and in an organized manner, you will be able to recall the article at a later date and improve your concentration, too.

VICTIMS OF A CURSE
by Art Buchwald

There is a great deal of soul-searching going on in this country as to why things have gone wrong. The Democrats blame the Republicans. The Republicans blame the radical-liberals. The students blame the Establishment. The Establishment blames Doctor Spock.

The one thing everyone seems in agreement on is that we're in a mess. The only thing no one is in agreement on is how we got into it.

I can now reveal the exact date and hour when things started going downhill in the United States. I can also reveal, for the first time, the reason why.

On November 10, 1958, at 11 a.m., a small brown package insured for $1 million was delivered to the Smithsonian Institution. Inside was the famous Hope diamond, a gift to the United States from Harry Winston, one of America's famous jewelers.

The Smithsonian was thrilled to have such a beautiful stone to display to the public. But what the American officials did not take into consideration was that the diamond had a curse on it—it brings bad luck to anyone who owns it.

Here are just a few of the things that happened to people who possessed the Hope diamond:

Louis XIV gave it to his mistress, Mme. de Montespan, and immediately abandoned her. The king himself contracted an incurable disease and finished his reign in disgrace.

The beautiful Princess Lamballe wore the diamond and was beaten to death by a mob during the French Revolution. Her head was paraded before Marie Antoinette, her closest friend. King Louis XVI, who inherited the stone, and his lovely Marie didn't fare any better.

The diamond was missing for several years. Then it turned up in the possession of Wilhelm Fals, a Dutch diamond cutter. Fals died of grief when his son Hendrick stole it from him. Hendrick committed suicide.

Francois Beaulieu, a Frenchman who owned it next, died of starvation after selling it to an Englishman, David Eliason, who sold it to an Irishman named Henry Thomas Hope.

The diamond was sold at auction to Jacques Celot, a jeweler who went insane and committed suicide. A Russian prince, Ivan Kanitovski, also owned it at one time. He was, as everyone knows, stabbed to death. Catherine the Great is said to have worn the diamond and she died of apoplexy.

After that it was just one bad-luck story after another. One of the female owners, after living high on the hog, was reduced to working as a scrubwoman for $2 a day in a shipyard.

A Spanish owner drowned in a shipwreck. A Greek broker who sold it to a Turkish sultan was killed with his entire family when his car went over a precipice in the mountains. When the sultan gave the gem to his favorite wife, she stabbed him. The McLean family, who owned the diamond before Winston, didn't come out of it too well, either.

The Hope diamond has brought nothing but grief to its owners, and whoever accepted it on behalf of the United States in 1958 did his country a great disservice.

Anyone who recalls what went on before 1958 and compares it to what is going on now knows we made a mistake. The question is: What is the solution?

One suggestion is that we present the Hope diamond as a gift to the Soviet Union. President Nixon could drop it off on his next trip to Europe.

If the Soviets refuse to accept it, there's always the Red Chinese. What better way of showing we want to be friends with the Chinese than to give it to Mrs. Mao Tse-tung to wear in her navel at the next rally at Peking Square?

Make comparisons

Whenever possible, read for the purpose of finding out how one body of knowledge compares with another. You take note of the similarities and the differences. If, in learning about electricity, you were studying transistors, you would see how transistors compare with the old-fashioned vacuum tube. After reading for similarities and differences, you would conclude your study by weighing the advantages of one against the other. In studying about different types of economic systems, you might compare socialism with capitalism, once again noting similarities and differences. You would divide the subject into categories, such as: how each system deals with private property, small business ownership, and so on.

Summary of purposeful reading

Remember that whenever you read, you are looking for certain information. You are in command of your attention. You are not to be helplessly beaten about by the printed word. Reading is an active process. It requires personal interaction on the part of the reader. Setting purposes while reading is new to most people, and it may require some self-discipline to break the temptation to read the supposedly shorter way. Yet the small investment in time that it takes to set purposes will bring overwhelming returns in terms of decreased daydreaming.

Generate your own thoughts

It is unfortunate that you cannot press a button in your brain labeled "input" or "receive" and record information the way a machine does. You should not be passive as forces act upon you. Maximum learning takes place when the input is met halfway. The good reader merges his/her own thoughts with the received information. Use your thought processes when gathering information. *Your* thoughts are just as valuable as those of the author. One of the surest ways to improve concentration is to generate your own thoughts before, during, and after reading.

Anticipating is one of the best techniques for improving concentration. By anticipating, you become personally involved. You respond emotionally. Certain nerve cells and pathways become "primed" to receive information. If you anticipate correctly, you get a feeling of satisfaction. If the author does not proceed as expected, it is no disaster. The mind has been all the more alert and attentive as a result of anticipating, whether it is proven right or wrong. Usually, a well practiced reader will be correct in his/her anticipations, and, as the speaker's words confirm his/her own thoughts, these thoughts become firmly imbedded in memory. If you have anticipated specific conclusions or reasons, and the conclusions are not offered, or are even rejected, by the speaker, you should be surprised. Curiosity should be aroused. You should spontaneously form more questions.

In the following selection, anticipate the main and supporting points of the author by reading only the first two paragraphs. Then look up and state what you believe the author is going to say. Then read the selection for the purpose of finding out: first, is your assumption correct? and second, do you agree with the author? State your thoughts clearly in full sentences, being sure to add why you agree or disagree. See if you can anticipate the supporting points as you go along. After so doing, read the entire selection. When you finish, state whether or not your anticipation was correct, and also, whether or not you agree with the author. Then answer the questions. You will be able to read faster and yet retain information.

THE NEED FOR BALANCE

Today Americans are more aware of the importance of clean air and water than at any time in our history. Also, we have made a good deal of measurable progress in this direction in the past decade. Much of the credit for achieving these positive results must go to those people called environmentalists. Without their urgings, we would not be as far along as we are. They can be justly proud of many of their successes.

But let us review some of the less fortunate results of environmental activities:

—Delaying the start of construction of the Alaskan pipeline for nearly five years means the U.S. will in the meantime have to import well over a billion barrels of oil that would otherwise have come from the North Slope. At today's high cost of foreign oil, this will create a drain of some $15 billion on the U.S. balance of payments. That's an extra $15 billion of the American people's money handed over to oil-exporting countries. Not to mention the increase of billions of dollars in the cost of the pipeline.

—The use of coal, our country's most abundant energy source, is being restricted severely in many areas by unnecessarily tight and inflexible limitations on sulfur content. This has forced large users to switch to low-sulfur heavy fuel, nearly all of which has to be imported—at very high costs.

—Construction and operation of nuclear power plants, which could have taken up some of the slack caused by insufficient domestic supplies of low-sulfur fuel oil and of natural gas, have been delayed.

—Legislation spurred by environmentalist lobbying has greatly increased U.S. gasoline consumption—by 6 billion gallons in 1974 alone —through emission-control systems installed on automobiles. Over the next three to four years the efficiency of automobile engines will drop still further, to meet that legislation's needlessly strict future standards within an arbitrarily short period of time.

—Every one of these actions placed an additional burden on oil supplies. At the same time, environmental pressures have delayed much of the increased offshore drilling that might provide some of the additional natural gas and oil the U.S. needs as a direct result of environmentalists' actions. This has made the U.S. just that much more dependent on other countries for high-cost, politically sensitive oil.

Another environmental achievement is the requirement that federal agencies prepare comprehensive documents known as environmental impact statements before they can proceed with offshore lease sales or grant permits for construction projects of any real size. Among other things, these statements have to discuss alternatives to the proposed action. Environmental impact statements do provide needed safeguards but have too often been used as an obstructionist tool for delaying energy projects.

Perhaps what the United States needs now is social and economic impact statements that would detail the social and economic consequences of *not* going ahead with any given project—for instance, the number and types of jobs that will *not* be created . . . the number of young people who will be *un*able to attend college if their parents are denied such jobs . . . the impact on the environment of insufficient supplies of energy to continue cleaning up our air and water . . . the increased dependence on foreign countries for oil . . . and the effects of this on the U.S. dollar, the international monetary system, and our country's economic and political security.

An adequate and secure supply of energy is not a discretionary item for our country. We have to strike a rational and workable balance between environmental risks and economic risks.

It seems to us that our country's failure to attain this balance reflects a normal human tendency of people to go too far (and too fast) in any given direction. We believe that, important as a cleaner environment is to all of us, it requires common-sense trade-offs. We believe timetables often can and must be made flexible even while one holds firmly to objectives. And we are convinced of the need to assess very carefully the economic and social costs to our fellow citizens of any proposed course of action.

Is all this to say that those of us in business have consistently been on the side of the angels, while the environmentalists have been on the other side? Of course not. People in business can be as wrong-headed as anyone. Certainly too many of us in business were slow to become fully aware of what had to be done to ensure cleaner air and water.

The problem is that over the past decade the pendulum has swung too far in one direction. Now, to mix a metaphor, we think it's time to balance the scales.

QUESTIONS:

1. Most low-sulfur fuels are
   a) proven environmentally hazardous.
   b) domestic, but extremely costly.
   c) imported.
   d) not in keeping with environmental standards.

2. Low domestic supplies of fuel could have been aided by
   a) low-sulfur fuels.
   b) oil.
   c) solar power.
   d) nuclear power plants.

3. Emissions control systems
   a) increased our consumption of gasoline.
   b) slightly decreased our consumption of gasoline.
   c) are effectively reducing pollution levels.
   d) enable cars to run more efficiently.

4. Environmental impact statements
   a) are rarely comprehensive.
   b) can be used as Communist propaganda.
   c) must be prepared before oil companies can raise their prices.
   d) provide needed safeguards.

5. By not going ahead with certain energy projects
   a) agriculture may suffer.

b) our society and economy will suffer.

c) the space exploration programs might suffer.

d) the labor force will be increased.

6. An effect of not going ahead with these projects might be
   a) reduced vegetable crops.
   b) a reduced number of jobs.
   c) an increased number of jobs.
   d) none of the above.

7. Standards for automobile pollution devices are
   a) needlessly strict.
   b) strict, but reasonable.
   c) too lax.
   d) pretty much in keeping with the needs.

8. Our country's most abundant energy source is
   a) natural gas.
   b) water.
   c) oil.
   d) coal.

9. There must be a balance between
   a) economic and political demands.
   b) economic and energy needs.
   c) energy and environmental demands.
   d) the use of oil and solar power.

10. A cleaner environment requires
    a) very strict standards.
    b) high fines for persons or industries violating environmental legislation.
    c) certain compromises.
    d) less dependence upon foreign oil.

ANSWERS:

1) c, 2) d, 3) a, 4) d, 5) b, 6) b, 7) a, 8) d, 9) c, 10) c

Construct a recall pattern

When approaching a chapter of semi-technical or technical material you have certain objectives. You wish to:

a) see how the author has organized the material.

b) set purposes.

c) skim over unimportant factual details.

d) prepare the brain to receive the information by thinking ahead.

e) start preparing for the moment when you have to recall and communicate the information to others, in an organized manner.

Here is a technique that will help you meet all five objectives.

Some people plod along word by word and then, immediately upon finishing the last word, close the book and exclaim, "I have read it!" They assume they will be able to recall. Others will do slightly better by rereading the key points. Others will do better still, by not referring to the material, but trying to summarize what the author said in their own words. Best of all, though, is to formulate the structure and sequence of ideas even before reading. In other words, to *prepare to recall* beforehand. You are going to prepare for the moment when someone asks you what a chapter said, before you begin to read the chapter. How can you prepare to recall a chapter when you haven't read it? It's easy, and in doing it you will simultaneously prepare the brain to automatically select what is most important. You will also be organizing your thoughts so you can read effectively and purposefully.

Construct what we shall call a "recall pattern" for the antebellum article. Imagine someone asking you what the article is about. Before even reading it you can make the general statement, "This section said that life in the antebellum period was characterized by nationalism," just from reading the titles. Do you know that many people could spend 30 minutes reading the entire chapter, and yet, when asked to recall it, would be unable to come up with this opening sentence?

You can continue your recall pattern. "Nationalism grew because, during that period, there was an increase in confidence." You now have formulated the second sentence in your pattern, the second sentence you would use to convey the information, and yet you have not yet begun to read. Notice that you are constructing sentences which delineate the organization of the chapter.

Underneath the heading "Confident America" are four paragraphs. Each paragraph contains one idea, perhaps a reason for the growth of confidence. The next sentence you construct might be "confidence increased because . . ." and you read *solely* for the purpose of completing your sentence. Once you realize that any paragraph below is not going to give a reason, you will quickly jump to the next one. That paragraph may add interest and flavor to the chapter but does not fit into the overall structure. Anything that does not help you complete your statements should be skimmed over. When you are reading strictly for pleasure and interest, you will want to read more of each of these paragraphs than just their main ideas. But if your objective is to read efficiently, and if concentration is a problem, then you will skip large portions of some paragraphs and the full text of others. If it is your objective to gain more factual depth, fine! You can turn back to the material. Once the basic pattern is formulated, review and study is greatly eased.

Many persons read similar articles and then are perfectly able to answer multiple choice questions or true/false questions afterward. When they are asked to give a written summary as in an essay-type examination, these same people are either totally at a loss for words or they come out with a hodge-podge of meaningless facts.

By scanning for specific information to add to a recall pattern, you are building the basis for a sound essay-type answer, one which is coherent and logically sequential. You will then be in a position to effectively convey the essential information of this article. At the same time, when reading to complete a recall pattern, you are also reading for better speed and concentration.

Review

Reading is an active, not a passive, process. At all times there is an interaction between the incoming knowledge and the memory of the learner. Review differs from reading in only one small respect—that the learner has considerably more material, more tools for interaction, than he/she did when reading the first time. The degree of interaction between learner and input knowledge can be thought of in terms of a scale. At one end of the scale is "recording." Here, the learner attempts to take in everything the way a camera or tape recorder does. The book and the learner do not interact. At the other extreme is "recitation." With this method there is also no interaction. The book is closed, or the reader looks away, and attempts to fish information out of his/her memory without aid from the book.

You can use different types and techniques of review, just as you can use different methods of scanning. The methods used for each depend upon the type of material, your level of knowledge, and your overall purposes. However, one basic principle holds true for all reviews, and that is that the review should tend to lean *more toward recitation* than the original reading. You should furnish more information from your own memory than you did when reading the article for the first time.

Recoding

Recoding is a form of recitation, with the difference being that you make up the recited information entirely in your own words. As a student progresses to higher levels of education, the importance of recoding increases, while there is a corresponding decrease in the value of pure recitation. In liberal arts courses, recoding ideally adds a measure of interpretation. Since you have opinions and attitudes about things, you organize the incoming knowledge in your own way. There is nothing wrong with interpreting some data subjectively as far as memory in general is concerned. Practically everything remembered is recoded to some degree.

Recoding is, in part, summarizing. While reading, you should look up after every page or two and restate in your own words the gist of what has just been covered. The ability to put much thought into a few words is very useful, both for permanent retention and for communicating ideas to others. Boiling knowledge down to a few words makes it more easily managed, and easier for others to listen to. If you can give concentrated, rather than diluted, material you can include more thoughts in a limited time and space. But it is too late to do this condensing at the moment you need to recall. You should begin the process while forming the recall pattern, and complete it in the review.

Write key words

Could you try now to recall all of the articles and excerpts that you have read thus far, including their major themes and supporting points? Needless to say, that would be quite difficult. However, suppose you are supplied with some key words or phrases such as: "Hope Diamond," "confidence," or "primitive tribes." You immediately start to recall information. Most likely other ideas and facts are coming to mind. You can see that the serial reconstruction principle works to recall reading material. Not only does a main idea recall supporting points, but one key word can start the chain effect by recalling the main idea. Is it true, therefore, that in order for you to learn how to remember any sequence of ideas, all you have to do is remember a list of key words? Yes, that is true! Therefore, to recall what you have read, obviously it is a helpful aid to have a few key words or phrases written down for any article or chapter. Usually the key word consists of either the subject or topic, or the action portion of the main theme. Later you can consult those words or phrases and they will do wonders for recall.

There remains an even better reason for writing, however. Just the act of having a pen in hand and being ready to take something down improves concentration immensely. Holding a pen tends to focus thoughts. If you take notes when listening to a speaker, you surely are aware of this effect. When you engage the pen or pencil, you are bringing the visual area of the brain into play. You are also bringing in the powerful motor area because you are engaging in a bodily action. You are now involving all of your mental faculties. It is well worth the investment in time to take down just a word or phrase from each idea that you deem worthy of retaining. When you are studying the "What Went Wrong?" article opposite, what key words or phrases might you wish to record? Perhaps "price controls," "search Alaska pipeline," "other energy sources," and "foreign oil." If you are careful while you read and study, these key words will remind you of all the main ideas.

WHAT WENT WRONG?

Mobil believes the nation's energy goal can be simply stated: In the coming decade, to produce a larger proportion of the energy we use; in the longer term, to achieve a reasonable energy surplus. Since nobody can forecast exactly how much energy the U.S. will need, it will be prudent to end up with too much rather than not enough.

But before we talk about surpluses, or even improved self-sufficiency, we have to ask: Why the present crisis? What went wrong?

The questions are necessary, because a nation should be able to learn from its past mistakes.

• *Mistake #1* is 20 years old. In 1954 the U.S. imposed price controls on natural gas shipped across state lines. In its eagerness to protect the consumer, the government focused on low prices for the short term. It gave short shrift to the consumer's long-term stake in security and adequacy of supply. The artificially depressed price of natural gas has produced today's shortage of natural gas, by stimulating demand while reducing the incentive to look for new supplies. Even under the best conditions, this shortage will be with us for years, and it will probably get a good deal worse before it gets any better.

• *Mistake #2* was the failure in past years to allow oil companies to press the search for oil and gas fully enough on the U.S. outer continental shelf. Reaction to the Santa Barbara spill caused too many people to lose their perspective. We must work to prevent spills and at the same time move ahead to try to assure adequate supplies.

Britain will be self-sufficient in oil about 1980, because it has actively promoted exploration under the seas around it, while the U.S. still puts "off limits" signs on thousands of square miles of outer continental shelf waters.

• *Mistake #3* was the failure to permit construction of the Alaska pipeline to begin much earlier. The pipeline raised legitimate questions about the environment. But scare tactics led to overreaction. Result: the line—designed to safeguard both terrain and wildlife on the basis of probably the most detailed ecological analysis ever made —was unnecessarily stalled in the courts and in Congress when it should have been pumping oil into the American economy.

• *Mistake #4* was the nation's snail's-pace development of other energy sources. Construction of atomic power plants has been delayed for a variety of reasons. Coal—our country's most abundant energy source—was clobbered from all sides. It couldn't compete with the artificially low prices imposed on natural gas (which in turn held down the price of another competitor, home heating oil), nor could it compete with low-cost foreign oil in the Fifties and Sixties. Finally, a lot of coal was made unusable by tight limitations on sulfur content.

Ironically, too, the *expectation* of cheap atomic energy discouraged investments in new coal mines—so that the country got the worst of both worlds. There were and are legitimate environmental concerns with both atomic energy and coal. But the nation has let itself be steered away from the basic question: "How much energy do we need, how soon, and at what economic and other cost?"

• *Mistake #5* was the naive belief by many that we could rely indefinitely on getting all the foreign oil we wanted at the price we wanted to pay for it—so that we could continue to waste energy and avoid correcting mistakes #1, 2, 3, and 4.

It could have been worse, of course. Remember the people who wanted to make the U.S. even more dependent on foreign oil, while assuring you that "national petroleum security" was a fiction devised by oil barons to keep domestic petroleum prices up? Remember the people who said not to worry about balance-of-payments problems, because these always righted themselves? And the instant tax experts eager to make sweeping changes, with little concern for the consequences? Fortunately, we didn't go all the way down any of those primrose paths.

Even so, for at least another 10 years, the U.S. is going to be heavily dependent on imported oil (coming increasingly from the Middle East), because of the long lead times that are unavoidable both in conserving energy on a large scale and in developing additional supplies.

To make a substantial reduction in energy use will require large investments by industry, new building standards for structures of all sorts, large numbers of low-horsepower cars replacing higher-horsepower cars year after year, the development of adequate public transportation systems, and other efforts.

It will take years, and very substantial investments, to discover and develop a new offshore oil field, or to get a new coal mine into operation or a nuclear power plant built.

Remember this when anyone tells you we can wait 10 years to even initiate any major effort.

Associate key ideas

Have you ever finished an essay-type examination or given a speech, and left the room with the gnawing feeling that you left out a large chunk of information? Yes, most problems in recall occur when you forget major topics. If you were only reminded of the topic, you could easily furnish a flood of details. The problem in memory is finding a starting point, finding one thought that will trigger others. If you have read and reviewed your material, only a phrase is needed. If you were given only the phrase "foreign oil," for example, would that prompt you to recall that the United States must increase its dependence on other countries for oil? Certainly not, if you studied your material. The phrase "foreign oil" would trigger the correct recollection.

You can remember a number of ideas in exact order if you remember words or phrases. To remember the key words or phrases that you have written down, tie the words together in the form of a story—a clear, vivid, crazy (if necessary) story that need not have anything to do with the information itself. Think of the energy crisis and what comes to mind? Waiting in line to get gas? Okay, use this vision, and connect it with the first phrase, "price controls." Imagine that you learn that the *price* of gas is *controlled*, so that it is too costly. So you *search* for gas yourself, going along the shore. You travel up the *Alaska Pipeline* and at the end run into *other energy sources* (an atomic power plant with coal in it). You fear an explosion, so leave on a ship carrying *foreign oil*. It may be ludicrous, but keeping this vision in mind is enormously effective as a memory technique. Later on, when recalling the energy crisis, the story and key words will come back to you. They, in turn, will recall additional information.

Imagine a use

Visual associations should be used when you are preparing for an essay test or a speech. Frequently, however, you may not know where or when the need to recall the information will arise. How often have you left a meeting or conversation in which the discussion touched upon a subject you had read about? Yet, it was not until later that you asked yourself why you did not remember and contribute the information when the subject came up.

Under the circumstances, you would not wish to make elaborate visual associations. You would like, though, to have a bit of information ready to furnish should the situation arise. The following procedure should be used to prepare for these situations: First, after finishing an article, imagine all the possible instances that would cause you to say something like, "Oh, I read an article on the subject recently. It said . . ." Suppose the article was entitled, "End of the Baby Boom." It reports the fact that fewer babies are being born in this decade, it gives a few reasons, and then it describes the effect this has on the nation's economic community. What uses for this information could you foresee? Under what conditions could you imagine that the need for your information would arise? Could you imagine the schoolboard meeting and someone suggesting the purchase of land for a new school? Can you imagine what you would say? Perhaps you could imagine an investor's meeting. Someone states that his stockbroker suggested he invest in a company that manufactures toys. What could be said here? What other such instances can you imagine? The more situations you can foresee, the more likely you will remember later on.

Next, visually construct each situation as clearly as possible. Mentally construct the setting, the people, yourself—everything—in a three-dimensional image. Last, see yourself conveying the information in the manner in which it should be communicated. Later on, if you have followed these easy, quick steps, any situation that just remotely resembles the ones you imagined will trigger your memory.

Keep reading records

A method of assuring retention over a long period is to keep records. Why not? Isn't knowledge and the time spent in acquiring that knowledge valuable enough to make sure the information is retained? It is very easy to record in a notebook information from books and articles. You don't have to write elaborate reviews. You don't even have to write a concise summary. Just a little outline of the author's structure will work wonders for long-range retention and recall.

There are many ways to outline and they are all good if they are comprehensive, yet short, and serve to recall other ideas. One method is to divide the paper into two sections, with the left side for main ideas and the right for supporting points or details. It may look something like this. Notice how finding organization is a natural part of this process.

END OF THE BABY BOOM
by Camille Bruce

MAIN IDEA	SUPPORTING POINTS AND DETAILS
Birth rate is declining	Statistics
Reasons:	The Pill Abortions Changing Social Attitudes a) more women valuing careers b) less of a stigma to being single
The economy may be adversely affected	Children's game and clothing companies going out of business
Business and Government must recognize and adapt to trend	Schools and hospitals will have empty spaces which can be used in other ways

Practice

a) Take any chapter in Part IV of this book and record it, applying the technique above.
b) Take a larger work of non-fiction and record each chapter in a similar manner.
c) Wait a month or more. Then review, using just your notes. You will see how effective recall will be.

For reading practice

Future Shock, a book written by Alvin Toffler, would be excellent for practicing the techniques (of organizing, discriminating, and forming recall patterns). Anyone who is interested in the mind (as you no doubt are, since you have read this far), should find this book absorbing. It describes how the fast-moving pace of modern life has made it necessary to learn and remember far more than we did in the past. At the same time we have many more opportunities and choices in our lives. Because traditional values and guidelines are breaking down, we must make more decisions on our own. All this, Toffler feels, is causing a growing burden on our mental mechanisms. He raises questions as to how well we can cope with this "ever-accelerating pace," and goes on to give suggestions for coping with the world of the future.

He makes many more points on a variety of subjects, and backs them with a remarkable amount of research, details, examples, and supporting points. While it all is quite fascinating and well written, there is one problem: If you try to read this book in the manner of the average reader, plodding through each word without pause or reflection, you will quickly be inundated with a barrage of facts. You can get a lot out of this book if you formulate a recall pattern. Once you can give an effective synopsis of each chapter, go on to the next. If you need more detail, or if one point particularly intrigues you, then by all means take steps to absorb it fully—but keep your purposes in mind.

how to remember numbers

Of all the areas concerned with memory, recalling numbers is probably the most difficult. Rarely are you presented with natural associations, as is often the case with names or facts. Also, numbers are very abstract. You could visualize the quantity two, for example, only if it were connected with an object. You could not, however, visualize 327 of such objects. You must use methods to change numbers into things that can be pictured and easily connected to information or to other numbers.

Here is an exercise that shows how this can be done: Memorize the 10 words below in order. Do not try to recall them by repeating the sequence to yourself. Instead, create a chain of associations. Visualize each word and associate it in a visual chain so as to construct a story. Make your story as wild and ludicrous as you can. Also, place yourself in the story. Start off by seeing yourself flashing a light and then throwing the light into a lake. Take it from there. After you have completed your story, test yourself.

1. light, 2. lake, 3. gear, 4. mare, 5. nail, 6. case, 7. bag, 8. cap, 9. rake, 10. neck

If you concentrated and chained all the words together, you probably remembered all 10 of them. If you did, congratulations! You have just memorized a 20-digit number. The number is: 14,106,737,210,586,087,020. You were able to succeed because each of the words is a representation of a two-digit number. This introduces the method which provides for the conversion of numbers into familiar and easily visualized words.

First transform each number into a letter. Use this code, for the following reasons:

0=K   O and K are often related; such as in "Okay" and "K.O."
1=l   The small letter l and the number 1 look similar.
2=n   Turn the 2 on its side and it resembles the n.
3=m   These are alike for the same reason.
4=t   The small t would look like a 4 but for one line missing.
5=s   They are nearly alike. A soft c sound can also be used.
6=G   These also look similar; a soft G or J sound can be used.

7=r	If the small r were turned around and straightened out just a little, it would resemble a 7.
8=b or p	The letter p on top of the letter b would make an 8 (Well, kind of).
9=d	The number 9 inverted becomes a d.

From here on the procedure is simple. By merely combining two or more of these letters and inserting vowel sounds between them, you can formulate words designating numbers.

Try this technique to remember telephone numbers. Suppose Sandy's telephone number is 896-5073. Convert the exchange 896 to b, d, g, which will make the word "budge" and 5073 to s, c, r, m, or "scram." Immediately the task becomes considerably easier because you can remember two words much more easily than seven numbers. If possible you could also compile all the information and form a vision of yourself telling Sandy to "budge," and then more forcefully, to "scram." You could also form a sentence with the first letter of each word carrying the information. Later on, if you have reviewed the association, the thought of Sandy will retrieve words or a sentence. From there, all that remains is the task of decoding your message. Thus, "Sandy *b*uys *d*umb *g*owns *s*o *c*osts *r*ise *m*iserably" could also be used.

You can also form names of persons or places or even combinations. Suppose you were trying to think of the phone number of a person you know named Kurt, and the phrase "Dennis in Senegal" came to your mind. What is Kurt's phone number? The answer is 925-5261. D N SS NG L

You may use actual letters in combination. For example, the license plate MBY 403 can be converted to MayBy To Ko Ma, and the telephone exchange of WA9 can be converted to WAD. Occasionally you will run into letter combinations that cannot make an intelligible word, but even nonsense words or sounds are more easily remembered than a sequence of numbers.

You may feel at first that it is simpler and easier to just remember numbers without going through all the bother of converting. Actually, if you practice and utilize this technique, you will see that there really is no comparison. You can have someone call out several telephone, license plate, or other numbers to you and associate each number to a person. Review your words or sentences once or twice. Then recall. It will be fun, and a good mental exercise.

NUMBER EXERCISE #1

Treat a number as factual information and connect it to a subject. This is similar to the technique for remembering facts, except that you must convert the numbers into a word. Remember these numerical facts:

1. James Polk was the tenth President of the U.S. Hint: You have ← LK

   an L on the left and a K on the right. Put a vowel sound in between. Then connect "lake" or "lock" to a pole.
2. The calorie count of V-8 ™ juice is 35. Hint: Change 35 to "mice" and associate. ← MC
3. The nineteenth amendment to the Constitution gave women the right to vote. LD
4. The atomic number of silver is 47. TR
5. The information about printing costs is on page 107. ▲ LKR
6. IBM stocks are priced at $269 per share. NGD

Review the previous facts:

It will be practical to have word conversions for numbers 1 through 10 firm in your mind. One of the countless uses of the words might be to remember a list of tasks or procedures in exact order. Following is a suggested list of word conversions. (At this point it is probably more important to understand the system by which the words are formed, rather than to know the exact words.) Notice that only the consonant sounds carry information. Silent b's or c's do not count.

TABLE OF CONVERSIONS

0	10	20	30	40
0 CAKE	10 LAKE	20 NECK	30 MIKE	40 TACK
1 COAL	11 LILY	21 NAIL	31 MAIL	41 TAIL
2 CANE	12 LANE	22 NUN	32 MINE	42 TIN
3 COMB	13 LAMB	23 NUMB	33 MAMA	43 TOMB
4 CAT	14 LIGHT	24 GNAT	34 MAT	44 TOT
5 CASE	15 LACE	25 NIECE	35 MICE	45 TOES
6 CAGE	16 LEG	26 NAG	36 MIG	46 TAG
7 CAR	17 LAIR	27 NERO	37 MARE	47 TEAR
8 CAP	18 LAP	28 KNOB	38 MOB	48 TUB
9 COD	19 LID	29 NOD	39 MAID	49 TIDE

50	60	70	80	90
50 SACK	60 JACK	70 RAKE	80 BEAK	90 DOCK
51 SAIL	61 JAIL	71 RAIL	81 BULL	91 DOLL
52 SUN	62 GUN	72 RAIN	82 BEAN	92 DEAN
53 SWIM	63 GUM	73 RAM	83 BOMB	93 DAM
54 SUIT	64 GATE	74 RAT	84 BAT	94 DATE
55 SISSY	65 GOOSE	75 ROSE	85 BASE	95 DICE
56 SAG	66 GAG	76 RAG	86 BAG	96 DOG
57 SORE	67 GEAR	77 REAR	87 BEAR	97 DEER
58 SOAP	68 JEEP	78 ROPE	88 BABY	98 DOPE
59 SEED	69 JADE	79 REED	89 BEAD	99 DEED

NUMBER EXERCISE #2

This is an exercise to remember five tasks in exact order. To remember the first, connect "coal" to making a withdrawal.

You might picture the bank teller handing you a bag of coal. When you recall, instead of mentally stumbling around for the first task, think first of your word for 1 (the same as 01 on the conversion chart). Now you have *a starting point* for recall. You picture coal by itself and the connected picture should remind you of making a withdrawal. Try to remember these tasks:

COAL 1. Make a bank withdrawal BANK TELLER HANDS COAL 01
CANE 2. Wash the car CANE is ON TOP OF CAR AS IS WASHED
COMB 3. Return a library book BOOK HAS COMB IN IT
CAT 4. Buy theater tickets CAT Buying TICKETS 03
CASE 5. Choose a birthday gift CASE HAS GIFT IN IT

RECALL EXERCISE #3 05

1. What is the atomic number for silver? T R
2. On what page is the information on printing costs? L K R
3. James Polk was what number President? (Notice the easy backward association.) L K
4. How many calories are in a glass of V-8 ™ juice? M C
5. What is the first thing in your list you must do? COAL
6. The second? CANE
7. What was the closing price per share of IBM? N G D
8. What number in your list is "return a library book"? COMB
9. What is the fourth task? CAT
10. The fifth? CASE

Check your answers! If you truly concentrated, you should see that using these word conversions can be a tremendous aid whenever a number must be associated with information. Be alert and you will see that the system has countless uses in everyday life.

Form a mental file

You can form your own mental file by having each digit of your reference number designate a certain category. Here is an example of one of the million uses of this system.

A real estate saleswoman explained her predicament with the following illustration: Mr. and Ms. Customer walk through the door and explain that they need a three-bedroom house. They estimate they can afford something in the $40,000 range. Despite having seen countless houses, the saleswoman cannot recall and describe a house that would be suited to this couple. She has no starting point for her thoughts, so she follows the usual procedure—she checks the files. Eventually, she finds a house that "fits" according to the description on the filed card. She felt, though, that it would create a more favorable atmosphere to be able to say almost immediately, "Oh yes, I have the house for you," and then give a brief description. Recalling the house from memory carries a personal touch, which is far superior to whatever comes out of a file. She must have a system that will enable her to reach into her vast mental storage and retrieve the most suitable house for any given combination of number of bedrooms and price.

Before you read the description of the procedure that she now faithfully uses, start with this basic premise: Any sequence of ideas, experiences, anecdotes, faces, or anything, can be recalled in a large part if you can first remember what is most important, what stands out or is unique, the "punch line," etc. The key thought that the saleswoman selects for association is the best physical feature of a house—the main selling point. If she can remember this visual picture, other recollections of the house will soon follow.

She forms a reference number by using the left numerical digit for the number of bedrooms and the right for the price range. Thus, a three-bedroom house in the $40,000 range could comprise the number 34. She then connects the *word* for 34 to the key selling feature of the house which is a beautiful porch. Later, when a couple walk in and say they need a house which falls into the above categories, she visualizes the word for 34 (mat) and in her picture, that mat is on a porch. Then other memories follow.

In this manner, the saleswoman has words to remind her of her favorite house, for houses having anywhere from one to nine bedrooms, and for prices from $10,000, to $90,000. Notice that when doing something like this, you could also add extra digits to indicate another category. Another digit, for example, might indicate the style of a house, or the presence or lack of a garage. The area is wide open for your creative thinking.

Learning the words

Success in using the word conversion system, of course, lies mainly in knowing the words backwards, forwards, and inside out. It would be embarrassing to make a large number of associations and then forget the words themselves at the time of recall. The words can be learned with surprisingly little effort. Once you have learned the basic system behind the formation of the words, you can and should *make up your own chart.* You can then compare your own product with the words used here, and make adjustments if you wish. If you come up with words different from those used here, it may be a sound idea to use yours as long as the basic system is followed. For a given number you should consistently use the same word. After you have done this, repeat the words to yourself a few times, and better still, use them at every opportunity.

Go shopping and remember 40 items by associating each item with the first 40 words of the chart. Why not also take bets? See if anyone believes you can do it!

Some quick ways of remembering numbers

I almost hate to include this section because I know that many readers will use these methods as a substitute for learning the word conversion system. I can only say once again that the word conversion system is devastatingly effective. With a little creativity, it can be adapted to countless situations. A few hours of practice will bring rewards for a lifetime, for the words can be used over.

You will occasionally not have time to form associations. In other cases you will wish to retain the numbers only long enough to use them shortly afterward, or only long enough to give you time to write the numbers down. All of the following suggestions will be helpful for these purposes:

1. You may find organization or progressions in numbers as was illustrated in Part I, Chapter 2.
2. Some numbers can be remembered as a date, e.g. 1957, 1546.
3. Visualize the numbers in three dimensions and vivid color.
4. Divide some numbers into dollars and cents. The zip code 15227 can more easily be remembered as $152.27.
5. You can perform a mental operation (thus employing the thought principle) on the numbers by simply adding them up. You can also use a combination of addition and organization. As an example, take the telephone number 587-6419. You total the left and right sides and get 20 for each.

Later on you will recall your mental operation. You may not recall immediately where and what all the numbers were, but your memory for the totals might be just the starting place that you need. From there you may suddenly be reminded of the complete number (as often happens in the case where the number has been used several times before but for that moment is unavailable for recall). Or you may find yourself remembering that it started with a 5 and ended with a 9. Then if you tell yourself that a total of 15 is necessary for the other two digits of the exchange, and 11 for the other three numbers, the forgotten figures may occur to you.

Have a joke-telling session and associate each punch line to a word conversion. Then see if you can recall the jokes in order. Of course the same technique could be used to remember paragraph numbers of rules, legal points, amendments, etc. Any idea can be associated using cues and the words.

CHAPTER 9

memory for communicating

How to Remember a Speech

The most important factor in remembering a speech is to recall the ideas or points—not just the words. The exact wording can always be extemporized, if necessary, if the ideas are recalled correctly. A formal speech should be well organized, so that one idea will recall the next. If your thoughts are well organized, the supporting points and facts will follow naturally. Writing the entire speech out will also be helpful in organizing your ideas.

In making your own organization, you should be sure to structure your ideas. See the speech as being comprised of a series of high points. As speaker, you must be aware that certain parts of the speech, certain points, are more important than others. You must discriminate on the relative value of your own ideas. As you proceed through the introduction to the body, and then to the conclusion, you must be aware of the key point in each portion of the speech. *Any time the mind discriminates, you enhance overall performance.*

After the speech is written out, recite it. Speaking into a tape recorder and listening to the playback will be extremely helpful. The most successful and convincing speeches are usually those that have been memorized. It is important, though, that you do not speak as if reciting from memory.

After you have demonstrated to your own satisfaction that you can recite the entire speech in the comfort of private study, you should then take steps to assure recall for the crucial moment when nervousness or distraction may cause forgetting. A good, clear, visual chain is usually best for this purpose, although letter chains, as well as combinations of the two, can be used. As speaker you should make a list of the main ideas in your speech, take cues or key words from these ideas and chain them together. You should be able to comprise a visual association of your main points, and should keep that picture before you as you speak. It is best to keep the association simple, containing only main ideas. The artificial association should not serve to recall the entire speech, word for word.

It would be foolish to construct a chain with a cue for every sentence, even though it could be done. The reason is that a chain that is too long or complicated will direct your attention and mental effort in such a way that the audience will note your detached expression. By keeping a simple but cohesive chain, you will remember the key points and avoid the possibility of getting "tongue tied" or of forgetting entire chunks of information. It is remarkably easy to visualize letter chains while speaking, but it does take practice. Most people will have no difficulty. If, though, you find a visual chain difficult, use letter associations.

Using letter associations

Letter associations are extremely effective in a speech, because normally a good speaker will need only a tiny hint, such as a letter, to remind him/her of a main idea. The letters will recall the key words or phrases that remind the speaker of a main idea. If the speaker has prepared adequately, these main ideas will in turn recall the examples, supporting facts, and points. Even if the speaker has not prepared thoroughly, or if the occasion calls for a more informal type of speech, the speaker should be able to extemporize, using these letters to recall the main ideas. The letters should prevent "mental blanks" due to nervousness.

Note the procedure. First, make a list of the key ideas or points. Then select a word or phrase that describes each idea. Choose a letter from each word or phrase, a letter beginning a key word. The letter will serve as a cue for recalling the word or phrase. Chain the letters together in a word that may or may not make sense. (As mentioned in Chapter 2, be certain to review what each letter stands for. Don't be afraid to overdo this step.)

The cue word should be kept in mind while speaking. To assure retention, visualize the word as well as repeating it silently. The word should be visualized in vivid color, quite large, and in three dimensions. Furthermore, the mind should once again discriminate. You decide which idea is most important, which idea you feel you surely wish to convey, and make it represent a large or a flashing letter, or both. One last word: while speaking, keep the mind active. Keep thinking ahead to the next point or to the next association. Do not let yourself be mesmerized by the sound of your own voice.

Memory in debates

Debating is a skill that requires considerable knowledge and practice. This book deals only with the aspect of debate that concerns memory.

As a speaker in a debate, you must reach into your storehouse of memories for arguments supporting your major premise. After the debate is over, it is not uncommon for debaters to criticize themselves, wondering why they had not countered with a particular point that was well within their sphere of knowledge. The problem is mainly in recall. When studying for a short answer test, you should think of all the questions that could possibly be asked on the test. By the same token, if you know you will soon be in a debate or argument, you should "prepare" to recall. You should anticipate your opponent's arguments, and rehearse answering them. You should be just as well acquainted with the other person's opinions as you are with your own. It often requires an added effort to understand opposing viewpoints, but the effort will prepare you better.

Once the debate is in progress, the mind must be active at all times. As soon as the opposition starts to speak, you should be anticipating the argument and be thinking of ways to counter. Occasionally, an opponent will wander to several topics when speaking, making it helpful to utilize a pad and pencil, jotting down points as the opponent speaks. When it is your turn, you return and cover the points. This way, you choose to answer those points in which you feel strongest, while disregarding others.

During a heated argument, emotions can become aroused. Normally this will not help your cause. Chapter 16 discusses how a high level of excitation can block proper transmission of neural impulses. It is therefore best to try not to become too emotionally involved. Assume instead a cold, analytical approach to the argument. Last but not least, it may often be helpful to prepare artificial associations for such information that you feel is likely to be needed. To be able to list a number of causes, statistics, or points from memory can be quite impressive.

Songs and poems

In memorizing songs or poems, too much attention is often exerted in remembering only words. Memory and enjoyment are enhanced when the full meaning of the words is understood. Therefore, before setting down to memorization, you should gain a full appreciation of the song or poem. If you want to remember a story, fix the progression of events firmly in your mind. You can usually form a clear visual picture of the proceedings. If the poem illustrates some philosophical concept, then the key lines or words should be seen in their relation to the overall idea.

The next thing to do is to break the poem into smaller units. People are best at remembering the beginning and end of things; the ability to remember falls off in the middle. This mental phenomenon is called the Serial Position effect. Taking this into account, you should turn attention to one stanza or section at a time, thus creating more beginnings and endings. Certain poems are exceptions here. If a poem is very cohesive, such as a narrative, if it is organized in such a way that to break it up into stanzas would interfere with the flow of thought, then it should be taken as a whole.

Then from each line or unit, take one key word and chain it to one from the next line or unit. Thus, for the poem below, you might divide it into four sections of two lines each. You might then think of the phrase, "too few spread dead." You are welcome to try and memorize the poem below, which was written just after the Battle of Gettysburg in 1863. First read it in its entirety a couple of times and project a full appreciation of the emotions the author wished to arouse. Get a feeling for the rhythm as well. (Rhythms can be helpful. Remember how you learned the alphabet through the alphabet song?) Then form other associations.

Do as much reciting as possible. You should be looking away and reciting, and referring to the print only when the associations and memory fail. This will mean looking back often at first, but less and less as you go along.

The muffled drum's sad roll has beat
The soldier's last tattoo;
No more on life's parade shall meet
That brave and fallen few.

On Fame's eternal camping ground
Their silent tents are spread,
And glory guards, with solemn round,
The bivouac of the dead.

—Theodore O'Hara.

Remembering theatrical lines

Normally the director of a play schedules an adequate number of rehearsals to assure that all members of the cast will have memorized their lines well. The only problem, insofar as memory is involved, is nervousness or stage fright, for these cause temporary mental blanks. Usually mental blanks on stage occur just before the performer must speak. It never happens during a lengthy soliloquy, but rather at the moment that the performer must enter his/her line.

Memorizing simple visual associations, pairing the performer's *first line* with the immediately preceding line, i.e. the last line of the preceding speaker, will rectify this situation. Just one key word from each of the two sentences may be used as the cues.

How to listen

Mind-wandering while reading can be caused by feeding the brain information at a rate that bores and distracts it. This problem is even more prevalent in listening inasmuch as our brains are capable of processing information at about four times the rate that people can speak. Inasmuch as the speaker can only say one word at a time, you can not rectify the problem by taking in groups of words, as you can do when reading.

Furthermore, to add to the difficulty, many lecturers will speak slowly and with long pauses. Sometimes several seconds may transpire between meaningful thoughts. When you must wait a few seconds between meaningful thoughts, you are, in effect, expecting your mind to go blank during that time. This can not happen in your waking state. Your mind will often refuse to tolerate this strain and will wander unless you take steps to help the speaker communicate.

What not to do

Many listeners will try to sustain attention by forcing themselves to repeat each of the speaker's words to themselves immediately after they have heard them. If you are able to keep this method up for as long as thirty seconds, you deserve a medal for determination. You certainly won't get anything else for your efforts. You are making no effort to make the words meaningful; all your mental power is concentrated on the wrong things. So the first thing to do is to relax and stop repeating the speaker's words like a parrot.

Mental Steps

KEEP YOUR MIND ACTIVE

The basic problem in concentrating while listening is that the mind has too much time to come up with irrelevant thoughts. If, however, the intervening thoughts were not irrelevant, but related directly to the lecture, then concentration on and memory of the speech would be greatly enhanced.

Bear in mind that a busy, active mind is best for listening. The more active a mind is, the more alert and receptive it is to receive information, assuming of course that the activities of the mind are related in some way to the presented information. An active mind does not get tired, the way a muscle does. There are numerous methods for a listener to keep his/her mind on the same wavelength as the speaker. All of the suggestions mentioned below will not only aid concentration, but will also improve comprehension and memory as well.

CLARIFY

It is unfortunate that we can not press a button in our brains labeled "input" or "receive" and passively record information like a machine. We can not be helpless as uncontrollable forces act upon us. We are in a constant state of change, and the knowledge we possess is due as much to our inner thoughts as it is to our environment. In humans, maximum learning takes place when the input is met halfway by the listener. The good listener merges his/her thoughts with the received information. Often this takes the form of clarifying what the speaker has said. Assume a biology lecturer states that nerves of the central nervous system (brain and spinal cord) do not regenerate if destroyed. You may then recall from previous lessons that nerves of the peripheral nervous system (arms, legs, etc.) can regenerate. It then becomes clear to you why a spinal injury can become very serious, often leading to paralysis. This new concept will surely be retained, because you have helped to formulate it. You have contributed your own knowledge to the subject. We remember our own thoughts better than anyone else's.

THINK OF EXAMPLES

You can involve yourself with the lecturer by thinking of examples. If the speaker tells you that the political atmosphere in America is changing, you can immediately think of examples to support his/her statement.

ANTICIPATE

Very often a good listener can anticipate the speaker's next point. Using an earlier example, for instance, the listener can anticipate the reasons why the political atmosphere is changing. The personal concern produces emotional reactions. You "prime" yourself to receive information and are satisfied when proven correct. Even if you are wrong, you have made your mind more alert and attentive. Although anticipation is the most difficult skill to practice, it is also the most effective for improving memory.

ASK QUESTIONS

Form questions in your mind while you listen. Seeking answers to these questions will be helpful in organizing your thoughts and in keeping your mind on a straight course. As a general rule, lecturers are happy to hear questions at any time during the course of a lecture, if the questions are sincere and genuinely related to the topic under discussion. Asking a question sometimes changes a discussion from a purely academic and impersonal affair to one that is highly personal and emotionally involving. Having formulated a problem and receiving a direct answer makes for a more powerful impression of the experience. This influences the way you store it.

SUMMARIZE

Speeches are usually not as well organized as are written words, and it is possible that lecturers may stray from the main theme. Nevertheless, the listener should strive to maintain a clear knowledge of the overall theme, purpose, or idea being presented. Periodically summarizing helps to keep the mind occupied, enhances memory by repetition, and helps to keep track of the speaker's ideas. Summarizing can be done in an incredibly short time. We can often think and recall our own thoughts at amazing speeds. This ability to think quickly enables you to carry on all these mental activities and yet still keep track of the speaker.

CRITICIZE

Develop the habit of criticizing. This does not mean that the speaker should be criticized personally, but that you should either agree or disagree with the presentation and know why you do so.

Lectures in the liberal arts and humanities always contain a human factor. They usually are presented in what is called a perspective or a slant. Topics in political and social sciences often evoke emotional responses. As an alert listener you should identify and sub-vocalize your feelings. Later on, you can start a chain of memories rolling back by recalling first whether or not you agreed with the speaker.

Taking notes

When all else fails, the average listener will resort to taking notes. Many students have discovered that note-taking provides additional benefit besides the obvious one of having a record for future use. They feel that writing somehow aids concentration. This is understandable. Writing keeps one's mind occupied, so that one has no time to deal with errant thoughts. The trouble in some cases, however, is that the students are often so busy trying to record the instructor's every word, that they are aware of only words and not thoughts. As a result, they do not really learn from the lecture. The learning must take place at some later date when the student has a chance to review the notes. By that point, much will be lost. Much of the information will be fragmentary. The context of some information will be lost. In addition, some of the important ideas will evade recording, as a consequence of the student's frantic efforts to keep pace with the speaker.

Note-taking is usually desirable but the student must find a happy medium. It would surely be a case of colossal conceit on the part of the instructor to expect that a student be able to regurgitate his/her exact words. Ideally, the student should get every main idea along with its supporting details, but not word for word.

If, when listening, you are properly applying the principles already discussed, you will be able to make a very good recording, and, at the same time, learn much from the lecture itself rather than by later reviewing. Studiously exercise the following: First, you should have a distinctive pattern or structure in taking lecture notes. The main ideas should be written largely and in full sentences (don't be skimpy with paper). Supporting facts and details, on the other hand, may be abbreviated as long as they are written below or beside the main idea. In this manner, the main idea will serve to recall the facts.

Be sure to isolate main ideas from supporting ideas in some way. Probably the best note-taking technique is to draw a line down the center of the page and reserve the right side for main ideas and conclusions and the left side for supporting ideas, facts, and details. When statements are received, you are forced to make a judgment about them. You must decide whether the statement belongs on the left, the right, or in neither place. Not only will it facilitate rereading of the notes later on, because the notes will be better organized, but the mere act of discriminating in this way aids concentration and memory immensely. (Note the technique of improving reading retention on page 80.) This technique also helps to make the mind more active. When you decide that a statement is a main idea, you are more apt to anticipate the next major idea.

One should be alert, however, to the possibility that the speaker may not be well organized, and that normal interruptions may cause some jumping from one topic to another. Make sure that enough space is left beneath a main idea sentence so that additional related data can be added should the speaker return to that point later on.

Listening requires practice

Anticipating, criticizing, summarizing, interjecting one's thoughts, thinking of examples, and asking questions, require quite a bit of mental work, but the outcome is worth it. You will retain not only what has been spoon-fed, but you will also have concepts that you have produced. It is, therefore, possible to leave a lecture and have obtained more knowledge than the lecture provided.

Listening is a skill and should be practiced and developed. It is not something that can be turned on once you learn the proper way to listen. Just because someone shows you how to do a new dance step does not mean that you will execute it properly the first time. The same is true for listening. You should sit down prepared to use all the methods of keeping the mind involved with the speaker, as well as to take notes. It will be extremely rare that all seven techniques can be used in any one lecture, but the better prepared you are to use all of them, the greater will be your chances of using some of them.

The interrelationship of reading and listening

This portion of the book discussed the utilization of several principles of concentration. Some were presented with reference to reading, others to listening. Actually, however, you should not say to yourself that "these are for reading, and these are for listening." A principle, by its definition, is broad, flexible, and far-reaching. At one time or another, all of the principles will be interrelated depending upon the organization of the reading material or lecture. Be critical of the written word whenever possible, and interject your own thoughts often. Periodically anticipate and summarize. Look for organization and purposes. Many good speakers will state their topic and main theme in their introduction, and the listener can then see what his/her purposes are. Principles of visualization and of emotional and personal involvement can be applied, of course, whether reading or listening.

Memory for conversational items

You have probably been told at one time or another that to have friends, you must be friendly. To get ideas across and persuade people, you must be able to understand others. In both cases, for successful human relationships, you must show interest in others. Now how often has this happened: You ask someone about his/her business or hobby. The person becomes animated and enthusiastic while responding. About 15 seconds go by this way and what happens to your mind? You are off somewhere, and the faraway look in your eyes does not enhance friendship or communication. So the next time you tell yourself, "Okay, I definitely will show interest this time." The person becomes enthused once again and this time, to make sure you show interest, you look the person right in the eyes—no blinking—no thinking—just looking. Some become expert at saying "I see" when they don't see, "very interesting" when they're bored, and so forth. Needless to say, these actions precipitate nothing but discomfort.

Memory over an extended period can be invaluable to maintaining friendships. Being able to come up with a statement such as, "Say, how is your son doing in medical school?" not only shows interest but is a good conversation prop as well. The previous section, though oriented toward the listener in a group situation, also applies to interpersonal communication. Your mind should certainly be active when you are engaged in interpersonal communication. It is also helpful to use association techniques on occasion. Most often, though, just being *aware*, and *selecting* items for reflection and retention will help.

Picture exercise

Now that you have studied association techniques in remembering names, facts, numbers, and conversational items, try to remember the following data about people, places, objects, and paintings. With each subject will be two or more items of information. Whether information is given to you in written, spoken, or visual form, start by making a selection. In each case, chain the items to your selection. Change numbers to words where necessary. Then, after a quick review, turn the page and test your recall. This exercise is difficult but you will remember if you give it your full effort.

Le Juene Marin I *(The Young Sailor) by Matisse brought $1,576,800 at a London auction on July 3, 1979.*

The Moons of Jupiter: Jupiter has a total of 13 natural satellites, including the heaviest satellite in the Solar System, Ganymede.

Pearl Moore of Francis Marion College, South Carolina, scored 4,061 points in her college career.

Oldest written language: This ancient Egyptian palette commemorating the victories of King Namer is over 5,000 years old.

Bugatti "Royale," type 41. First built in 1927; has an eight-cylinder engine of 12.7-liter capacity, and measures over 22 feet in length.

memory for daily activities

Remembering Those Little Things to Do

Everyone has had countless instances in which he or she "forgot" to bring along some item, to relay a message, or to turn off the parkway at a desired exit. These are all examples of forgetting "the little things." I truly must question whether or not these mishaps should technically fall into the category of "forgetting." Forgetting occurs when you consciously make an effort to remember and then you fail. In forgetting "the little things," on the other hand, the problem is usually one of timing. You were busy thinking of something else (perhaps you were busy talking while passing the exit) at the moment when you should have been reminded of the proper action. Taking another example, consider the high school student who was about to play in her first varsity basketball game and upon getting suited up, realized that she had forgotten to bring her sneakers. Now surely the young woman did not forget that sneakers are necessary for basketball. The question simply was not raised to her. She did not think of the sneakers at the proper time. It was really a problem of, what might generally be described as, "personal organization."

Nevertheless because people are accustomed to viewing these errors in timing as a problem of memory, and because the problem of forgetting these "little" things plague all of us to some degree, and because the principles already touched upon will help alleviate the problem, here is an examination of this topic.

Memory and personal organization

The principle of organization is very important in remembering reading or lecture material, as you have seen. Organization relates to all aspects of successful mental functioning. It is no coincidence that people who describe themselves as disorganized also describe themselves as being forgetful of those "little" things to do. It is easy to understand why the organized person is less likely to forget things. The organization-minded person unwittingly has gotten into the habit of applying principles of memory. For example, the organized person makes a list of things that he/she must accomplish in a given day or week. Often this list will start with the most important chore and gradually work down to the least important. Just the mere act of making the mental *discrimination* that decides the relative importance of each chore aids memory. Furthermore, the act of writing utilizes the kinesthetic areas of the brain, thus providing an extra avenue for recall. After performing these mental operations, a person may not even need the list any longer.

The organized person is less likely to forget to bring items with him/her in the morning because he/she usually prepares the items the night before, when mental activity and interference are on a lower level and the likelihood of forgetting is decreased.

Recognize your crucial moments

Suppose Ms. Businessperson is about to leave the office. As her hand touches the doorknob, something reminds her that she must make an important phone call. She calls and is thankful that she "remembered." Now assume this woman is in the comfort of her home. It is after business hours, too late to make the call, and now some recollection of the phone call comes to her. What does she say to herself now? You guessed it! "I forgot!" she says, despite the fact that the recollection was the same. The only differences were *time* and *place*. Whether or not you forget to do something often depends upon when and where you "remember." You probably often remember things too late, and call it "forgetting."

In everyone's day, some moments are more important than others from the standpoint of memory because, if you have failed to remember something, the time and place of these moments will remind you of what you had forgotten. For many people, that crucial moment is right before leaving the house in the morning, or right before leaving the job at 5 o'clock. If you remember just at these moments, you will get whatever it is done; if not, it will be forgotten. Therefore, these are key moments in the day.

Ask yourself which moments are crucial in your daily life and get into the *habit* of checking at that time to make sure you have not forgotten anything. The fifteen or less seconds that it may take will be well worth it.

To remember for the future

Often it is necessary to remember to do something in the future. Perhaps, as you begin your trip, you remind yourself to turn off the parkway at a certain exit. Or you want to remember to give a co-worker a report when you see him, not suddenly to recall after he has left and it is too late. You say things like, "Sure, I will call you tomorrow night." This section discusses how to follow through with your intentions.

Memories come back to use through mental interrelations, as stated earlier. An object or event taking place in the present reminds you of something in the past and triggers a stream of memories. Often some object or event in the present taps your memory storage, reminding you of things to do. Wouldn't it be nice if you would always have an object or event to remind you to bring along something, do a chore, or make a correct turn off a parkway?

Treat the forgetting of little things to do as due to errors of timing. "Forgetting" to turn off the correct exit of a parkway occurs simply because you were not thinking of the right thing at the right time. What is needed here is some event or object that will somehow appear shortly before the desired exit and will serve to tap your memory storage, snapping your mind back to the situation at hand. Imagine driving along the parkway and running into a gigantic traffic jam caused by a terrible accident. As a result of the jam you must turn off the highway at a certain exit. Do you think that the next time you approached the spot where all this happened, you would be reminded of the incident? Yes, most likely you would. The place would trigger the memory of the experience. This memory would serve nicely to remind you to turn off the parkway at the next exit if you wished to do so.

If you want to make sure that you turn off at a particular exit there is no need actually to have been in the gigantic traffic jam. You can *create the experience* yourself. You can create a visual experience of the accident, using vivid color, exaggeration, and all of your imagination. If you are at all familiar with the road, you can imagine the incident occurring at a specific point. A bridge, tunnel, park, etc., shortly before the exit will do fine, because these are things you will surely see. Well in advance, when you determine that you will need to turn off at a certain exit, you select a landmark that you will see before the exit, and imagine a huge traffic jam there and having to turn off. Later, when you are driving along and your mind is occupied with various thoughts, and you come to that bridge, you will be reminded of the "incident," and you will then think about making the correct turn.

You can imagine a scene to remember *anything*, as long as you know in advance what you wish to remember. Suppose you want to make sure that when you see an office co-worker you remember to give him some written information. You create an incident, the more exaggerated, wilder, and crazier the better. You can picture yourself giving him the information, him getting red in the face, jumping up and down, pounding the desk and screaming, "My God, how I needed this. Do you know what could have happened if I didn't get this?" You could then picture him fainting and you having to call a doctor. Later, all you have to do is set eyes on the person and you will immediately be reminded of the created incident, which will remind you to give him the information. In actuality he may accept it with hardly a trace of emotion or comment, but that is beside the point.

The procedure can be summarized as follows: First, decide on whatever it is you want to remember. Second, pick out some object, place, or person that is closely associated with it in time and place; and third, create a ludicrous memory of some event in which that object, place, or person is a central figure. To make the technique slightly more effective, the event may also bear some relationship to the desired task, although that is usually unnecessary.

To remember a large number of tasks

Some of us are in business or social situations that necessitate the retention and recall of a large number of tasks, say five or 10, each day. Under these circumstances it may be time-consuming and mentally congesting to create wild memories for each and every little chore. If you live with this situation, you can still utilize the technique of creating memories that serve to snap your mind back to the desired task at the right time. The only difference is that you should omit the absurdities. Simply create the memory of yourself performing each task in the exact environment at precisely the same moment that you expect to accomplish the task, but omit the extras. In other words, if you wish to give a co-worker a letter, simply create a sharp picture of yourself giving it to him. Create all the circumstances as you actually expect they would be. Later you will remember even if the circumstances differ somewhat. This technique will be almost as powerful as the preceding and yet will be effective for those with busy, or even hectic, lives.

When the time is indefinite

"Okay," the forgetful one may ask, "this is all fine when you can know where you'll be in the future, and you know exactly when you want to do something. But what about those instances when you know you should do something but it doesn't have to be done at any special time or in any particular place?"

Yes, intentions stated in matters such as, "I must call my sister this weekend," or "I will write the letter tomorrow," or "I shall cash the check today," are often forgotten. These statements of intent are really the killers. Which statement do you think will be remembered? A: "Take this pill once per day," or B: "Take this pill after every meal." B is the correct answer. The meal will be a reminder.

It is precisely this lack of a definite time and place that is the very cause of so much forgetting. If you know exactly when and where you are to perform a task, the occasion itself will often remind you of the chore. When no exact time and place is designated, chances of recollection are slim. The implication then is clear. If the chore does not require a definite time and place, you must *select* one. You must state *exactly when* and *exactly where* you will make the telephone call or mail the letter. Just the mere act of discriminating, picking out one from the multitude of occasions that you interact in, will sharply reduce the chances of forgetting. After you have made your selection, you may then create an experience as outlined in the previous section.

Remembering Where You Put Things

Talking to yourself can help immensely—not after you are already beside yourself with despair, but when you are putting the object in its place. It will be helpful to add a reason for your putting something in a particular place. If you have a logical reason for putting something somewhere, vocalize that reason. Even if there is no special reason for your dropping the object in a given place, it would help to make up a reason and vocalize it. "I am placing the baby pictures in the dresser because the dresser is occupying the spot where the crib was located." You will remember your own thoughts and words.

Even more effective will be your own body actions. When you put something away, add a physical movement. Add a little extra flip when you put an object on a table or desk. If you put something in a lower drawer, kick the drawer closed. If you are alone, there is no problem with this. If, on the other hand, you are concerned that someone may think you are crazy, then push the drawer closed with the back of your hand, or place the letter on the table with a gentle pat instead of a mighty whack. Later on, just visualize the object you have put away and your action will be remembered. This, in turn, will recall the location.

Memory For Card Playing

Remembering the cards that have been played is not as difficult as it seems under normal circumstances. The underlying problem really is concentration. It is impossible to close your eyes and think of absolutely nothing. With your eyes open, though, if you have something visual to look at (cards, for example), it seems that your mind can go blank. You can remember much more if you just keep your mind active. When playing a game that requires some memory, just keep the brain working and visually reviewing the play of the cards. Your mind can work much faster than people can play. Make use of that fact.

It may be difficult to maintain full concentration while playing cards. Certainly in poker it is easy to be distracted by thoughts about money, and not give full attention to the cards. Consider the bridge player who has a funny feeling that he is botching up the play of the hand—and he also has the feeling that the kibitzers looking over his shoulder *know* he is botching up the hand. Perhaps he also thinks of what he will say to his partner when the game is over. Learn to recognize when the mind is off on useless thoughts while playing, and get in the habit of immediately bringing the mind back to the game.

Of course it would be possible to construct some method of mnemonic association to remember cards, but, while mnemonics are perfect for many problems concerning memory, for practical purposes a mnemonic method to remember cards would create more problems than it would solve.

Keeping the mind moving is the best technique. Never miss chances to mentally review the cards already played. Consider all possible outcomes and consequences. Bridge players will notice that the best players of that game remember the cards after the hand is over. That is because the good players have done more thinking that relates to the play of the hand.

Memory for Athletics

Perhaps the most spectacular demonstration of communication, cooperation, control, and coordination is achieved when literally thousands of nerves, muscles, and chemicals join forces in the successful execution of a golf swing, a dance step, or another sophisticated movement. It would take an oversized book to describe in detail how each component part performs its function in perfectly timed sequence.

The brain controls physical as well as mental operations. The execution of skilled movements is a mental activity just as surely as it is a physical one. A skilled movement properly executed is knowledge. It calls for learning. When you are called upon to perform the movement, successful recall is necessary. To enhance both learning and memory of the movement, the person engages in repetition, or in other words, practice. You can see, then, that skilled movements in athletics or related areas are partly a function of memory.

Consider the problems of learning a complex body movement. For example, a beginning student of tennis prepares to hit a basic forehand shot right after receiving instruction. She may have learned well enough to swing correctly in practice—that is without the ball being hit to her. But now comes the moment of truth. The ball is about to be lobbed to her. Somewhat lacking in confidence, she frantically tries to tell herself what to do by mentally reviewing the instructor's words. She tells herself to keep the arm extended, transfer the weight from right foot to left, meet the ball slightly in front of her, etc. Then the ball is hit, rather easily and in perfect position, but what transpires looks more like a karate chop than a forehand swing. It may be concluded that she simply forgot the proper form when the ball was hit to her.

Similar problems in recall are typical of the great majority of athletes in competitive, pressured situations. Basketball players, from schoolyard to professional ranks, shoot less accurately on foul shots in games than they do in practice. They score a lower percentage because in an actual game their bodily recall is more subject to interference due to distractions and tension. The problem of comparatively poor execution of complex body movements under certain conditions will be regarded as a problem of memory. Treat it in accordance with the two principles discussed in Chapter 2, visualization and ego involvement.

Here is a situation that applies these principles. The golfer approaches the tee and prepares to recall. He does this not by repeating words of instruction to himself, but by *visualizing* the correct procedure. He visualizes the correct swing in its entirety, from the backswing to the follow-through. He is sure to recall, at this moment at least, because if any part of the proper motion is left out, the vision will not look right. Next comes the principle of ego involvement. We remember things that happen to ourselves. Therefore, in the image, the golfer visualizes himself making the correct swing. He does so from two viewpoints. First, he visualizes himself from the viewpoint of a spectator, and second, he visualizes how everything will actually look when he swings. He even tries to remember what it feels like to swing correctly, thus activating the kinesthetic area. And because we are normally inclined, or should be inclined, to remember our successes rather than failures, it is best for the golfer to include a ball in the image. He sees himself swing perfectly, sees himself make perfect contact with the ball, and sees the ball take off for a beautiful shot.

Basically, the same principles can be used to remember any skilled act in which partners or opponents are not too much of a factor in the act's execution.

CHAPTER 11

how to study

This section is basically for the student. However, with the ever-accelerating knowledge explosion of the modern age, it is becoming increasingly apparent that good study habits are an asset at any age. Anyone who applies the principles and techniques in the chapters on reading, listening, and remembering facts will undoubtedly be an excellent student. Nevertheless, there are a few concepts to add to this subject.

A basic study method

George, an average student, approaches a chapter by saying, "I have got to read this." He then plods through, saying each and every word to himself, ignoring headings, subtitles, graphs, illustrations, and questions posed by the author. As soon as his eyes arrive at the finish line, the ordeal is pronounced over, and he exclaims, "I have read it," and closes the book. If anything, by now you should be able to see that learning is complicated. Study requires not only skill, but a plan of attack. There are no easy answers in determining an exact approach. Assignments vary in degree of difficulty, length, and depth of knowledge expected by the instructor. Furthermore, individual students' characteristics vary even more than the assignments. Therefore, only a general plan will be presented, bearing in mind that within each of the steps below there is plenty of room for variation.

The method can be broken down into four general steps: prepare, read, memorize, and review. Whether studying for business or academic reasons, this basic plan of attack can be used.

Methods of Preparation

Skimming

Part of this first step entails finding out what is to be expected in the way of input knowledge. Upon completion of skimming, you should know enough about the assignment to be able to see a use for the knowledge, and to set the stage for a little thinking on the subject. At the same time, you should divide the assignment into smaller parts, and set reasonable goals for completion.

There are many ways to skim. One way is to force your eyes to travel down the page as rapidly as possible, picking out key words or terms. This method is good when there are no subtitles and the reading is rather light. It takes considerable practice, however. Another technique for non-subtitled reading is the one outlined earlier: reading the first and/or last lines of paragraphs, reading the first and last paragraphs fully, and reading any chapter summaries or previews. When there are many divisions of headings and subtitles, preparation is easier. Reading summaries plus searching for just the main idea of each subtitle may be more than sufficient.

Scanning for interest

Very often the best approach is to simply cruise through the chapter, searching for points that arouse curiosity. You can use this method for any type of material that is organized in such a way that comprehension does not depend on the mastery of preceding points. Learning is at its utmost when motivated by curiosity. Many students will see something of interest and then interrupt themselves, saying, "I shouldn't bother to read this now. I'll get to it eventually." This is a poor practice. Anytime you are interested in learning anything, you should not deny this natural learning state. This condition often will not return. Scanning in this manner is extremely effective, pleasant, and effortless, as long as you are careful not to get bogged down. Once your curiosity is satisfied, do not keep reading, but quickly go on to the next topic.

"But what if I do not find anything of interest?" the student may ask. Well, this would be very unfortunate if true. Quite often, however, by scanning in this way, you will find that you have more interest in your work than you thought. Everyone is interested at some times more than others. The problem is that if, as so often happens, you get in the habit of looking upon school or work relating to your occupation as a chore, then you do not allow yourself to freely enjoy your material. If you assume that a subject will be boring, and start with that assumption, it surely will be boring. In releasing yourself to respond wholeheartedly to the subject, both intellectually and emotionally, you will be more likely to find joy in the work.

Read the questions first

One of the easiest and best ways to set purposes is to read questions, if they are provided at the end of the chapter. In reading, you then set out to find the answers. Most students ignore these questions at the end unless they are assigned. Actually, they can be of immense value in getting the mind set on a straight course.

These questions normally cover the points that the author feels are important and usually the author and instructor are in agreement.

You may feel that the questions were placed at the end because they were meant for reviewing and should be used for that purpose. It may be true that the author's intention was to provide these questions for review. However, any author is more concerned that his/her work be read and understood. Review is a considerably easier chore than reading a chapter for the first time, especially from the standpoint of concentration. The student should use any means—visual aids, pictures, summaries of material, anything that will help establish purposes while reading.

Prepare by writing

The technique for keeping reading records, discussed on page 80, is an excellent study aid. Use this method for outlining a chapter. One further word here: try to write as many general statements as possible beforehand. That way, the lesser ideas will more easily fall into place.

Prepare yourself

Equally important, you should prepare your entire self to absorb the information. This means clearing your mind of all worries or distractions before you sit down to study. Little tasks or decisions should be dealt with *beforehand*, thus freeing the mind for more important matters.

You should try to get into the habit of studying at a particular time. Morning is generally better than evening, as these hours usually have fewer distractions. Even if you do force yourself to stay home and study in the evening, the night hours often become associated with socializing or other activities, and a time or place can trigger unwanted thoughts as well as desired ones.

Finding organization

After skimming the material, the author's organization should be firmly in mind, and it should be kept in mind when you later start reading. Last but not least, with good preparation the student should know how fast to read the chapter in general, and which parts are the most important.

Time for preparation

It is reasonable to wonder how much time should be spent in preparation. Frankly, there is no exact answer that applies equally to all students and all texts. However long it takes to accomplish the objective just outlined is the proper amount of time. Sometimes, a good preparation can take but a few minutes with most of that time spent in thought. Sometimes, thought alone, stating what you think the chapter will tell you, will suffice. On other occasions, *it will be necessary to spend more time in preparation than in actual reading*, and there is nothing wrong with that.

Read

After sufficient preparation, you should read rapidly with considerable involvement. Not much more can be added here that has not already been discussed and practiced. Remember that the objective in reading is merely to *build upon the foundation of knowledge that you already laid*. You are just seeking more depth.

Examinations

Basically, there are two methods of testing knowledge of written material. One is the short-answer type, which includes multiple-choice questions, true-false questions, and sentence completions. The other is the written or essay type, where the information is expected to be communicated in written paragraph form. The short-answer type is usually more difficult because specific facts are called for. Students typically fear the essay type more, however, because it is a better test of memory. It also calls for a logical construction of ideas. If you follow the procedures in Chapter 2 on association techniques, utilizing the recall pattern construction discussed in Chapter 10, you should have no trouble with essay-type tests. If you are studying periodically for a comprehensive written examination that tests knowledge attained over a period of months or even years, the suggestion for recording knowledge, on page 80, should be particularly helpful. For the short-answer type examinations there is another technique that has not as yet been discussed— self-testing.

Self-testing

Many people judge their knowledge of a chapter on the basis of whether or not they have read it. When confronted with a sudden unscheduled quiz, most students first ask themselves whether or not they have done the assigned reading. Whether or not they *know* it is not their immediate concern. Judging your level of knowledge by how much you have read is similar to basing a basketball team's score on the number of shots taken, or determining the number of miles driven by the time spent in the car.

Despite the absurdity of considering a subject as known simply because assignments have been read, many students do just that. Perhaps they succeed in clearing their consciences by just reading. If they do poorly on the examination, they blame their poor memory, not the fact that they never really knew the subject.

It is often amazing to note the extent to which people overestimate their memory ability, whether it be in study, remembering people's names, or remembering things to do. After having learned something, people assure themselves that they couldn't possibly forget, and tend not to see the necessity of review. The more you reflect on this matter, the more obvious becomes the need to test yourself as an integral part of review. In self-testing, the objective is to find out how much you know and how much you do not know, by asking yourself questions on topics and then reciting to see how well you can answer them. It is not necessary to recite out loud, but recitation means verbalizing the answers at least silently. Often in self-testing, one finds that one's knowledge is not as clear on a subject as one thought it was, and one takes steps to correct the situation.

Studying for the short-answer test

Students working together can help each other immensely by each taking turns posing questions to the other. Do not fear that this method means that some time-wasting is involved. Actually, the person doing the questioning will gain just as much from picking out questions and judging answers as will the one being tested. You remember the sound of your own voice.

Short-answer-type tests in particular should be reviewed largely by the method of finding questions and trying to answer them. It is not necessary to work with others. Working individually or with others, the best reviewing technique for short-answer tests is to imagine yourself as the teacher. Then you look through your reading assignments and pick out questions that you feel should be on the test. You single out those questions which, combined with their answers, contain the most important information in the paragraph. Seeking questions helps one to employ automatically much of that which has been discussed in this book. Make sure to review in this way. The results can practically be guaranteed.

Review

Review comes last, to be sure, but that does not mean review should not take place before the assignment is fully read. You should look up on many occasions, and either recite or recode to make certain of your understanding and to enhance retention. Also, if you notice good questions or important points, mark them.

The acts of recitation, recoding, and repetition were all discussed in Chapter 4. All of these processes should be employed when studying, although the proportion of time spent on each should vary with the circumstances. Repetition, simply re-reading, is to be used whenever understanding is uncertain, or when, after self-testing, you realize that you have forgotten something. Recitation and re-coding can easily be confused in practice. Generally speaking, the broader the knowledge, the greater the proportion of review that should be spent in recoding. Thus, liberal arts usually call for re-coding, while technical and scientific study call for more recitation. Memorization of artificial associations and cues calls for pure recitation.

Do most interesting assignments first?

Students are often advised to tackle the least-favored or hardest subjects first, saving the easy or interesting one for last. Very often people accept statements and well-meaning advice un-questioningly. Frankly, I must seriously question this grueling approach to a study session. Study should not be regarded as a chore. As noted, an individual works best when he/she has completed assignments and gained a measure of satisfaction. By tackling and finishing the easiest assignment first, the student can then approach the next one in a better frame of mind.

More important, however, is the aspect of curiosity. The great French philosopher, Jean Rousseau, built an entire educa-tional philosophy on the basic premise that people are born with a natural desire to obtain knowledge. However, this is only a potential. All innate potentials are formed, molded, and sometimes even des-troyed by our life experiences and patterns. The two-year-old child who is consistently punished for touching things in the house in his quest to learn, will not seek knowledge later on.

Sincere curiosity is an emotion and it is precious. It must be nurtured whenever possible. To put off some interesting scholastic material for something less so, amounts to a flagrant denial of your mind's natural quest for knowledge. *You learn best when motivated by curiosity.* When curious, you have certain ques-tions which you believe will be answered by your reading. You have a clear and specific purpose. During these moments, you concentrate better, work efficiently, and remember more. Curiosity, like any other emotion, has high and low points. A person may be quite inquisitive at one moment, and less interested the next, whether or not the curiosity was satisfied. You should study when you are interested because that is the best time to learn and that optimum moment may take a while, if not forever, to return.

The frame of mind you have when approaching study, whether positive or negative, is very much a result of your attitudes and is determined in part by your prior learning experiences. If you habitually regard study as something to be endured or as a sort of punishment for living, if natural curiosity is always denied in favor of a rigid routine, your capacity to be curious will gradually decrease.

When to study

In college, the student has considerable freedom to decide when to study. Ideally, it is best to spread study more or less equally over a period of time, for example, reviewing frequently over a semester. But, let's face it! Most of us respond to a call of urgency: a test or meeting for instance. We do most of our studying shortly before the final examination. There is nothing wrong with a solid several hours of study before a test. However, the study at this time should consist mostly of review. There should be at least some familiarity with the material.

Preparing for class

In most college courses, the reading assignments parallel the lectures or class discussions. Often classes are wasted in daydreams because the student does not know enough about the subject to follow the lecture. For this reason, maximum efficiency is attained by preparing for the class. It is not necessary to know the material backwards and forwards at this time. Just enough knowledge to think intelligently about the material will do wonders. You will then make the most efficient use of class time, and be more adequately prepared to perform the listening skills discussed in the next chapter.

Occasionally, the reverse procedure is also of value. The student first listens to the lecture, and then, fortified with a good base of knowledge, is better prepared to tackle the textbook shortly afterward. This order should be applied only if concentration or comprehension of the textbook would be difficult without some introduction or explanation, or if a student is an exceptionally good listener. An excellent procedure to follow is to go through the preparation stage *before* class, read thoroughly shortly after the class, and memorize the review before the test. Once again, there is much leeway, but a systematic schedule should always be employed.

Introducing Part III

Thus far, you have seen how to get information and ideas into memory. This is the most important part of memory improvement from a practical, everyday standpoint. The next section discusses some additional factors that determine how long you will be able to keep the information, and how you can draw upon your memories when you need them.

part III
retention and recall

CHAPTER 12

why and when people forget

Forgetting cannot be avoided. If you didn't forget, your mind would become hopelessly cluttered with useless information. Your life is constantly changing, and this calls for adapting to those changes. Forgetting allows you to stop remembering what is no longer useful, thus enabling you to absorb new information.

The problem in forgetting is not the fact that you forget, but that you forget certain things you have made a conscious effort to remember—things that you know are important. The problem is that the mechanism of memory works independently of conscious thought. The conscious mind is certainly affiliated with the memory mechanism; it affects memory by its power to direct attention. But the conscious mind does not control memory. You cannot consciously determine just what will be remembered and for how long. You can finish a chapter of required reading and say to yourself: "I must remember what I've just read because I will be tested on it," but that determination alone does not guarantee that the chapter will be remembered.

Deciding that something is worth remembering is no more effective, at times, than deciding to fall asleep or not to blush. In such situations other mental factors enter into the picture, factors that are beyond your conscious control. If memory were subject to your conscious desires, you would have a more difficult time than you do now. You would have to interrupt your thoughts and actions constantly, in order to decide whether or not you wished to remember each detail of your daily experiences. Your brain has worked out methods of deciding what is worth remembering without the aid of conscious thought, so that you can turn your attention to other aspects of life. For the time being, then, be thankful that your memory system is just the way it is. Look upon memory as a systematic organization which is subject to general but consistent guidelines in its selection and retention of data. A careful analysis of these guidelines will help you understand why things which you believe important are often forgotten. This understanding will play an important part in your memory improvement.

The Theory of Interference

It is commonly believed that the key factor in forgetting is the passing of time. The more time that elapses between when you learn something and the moment you wish to remember, the less that will be recalled. While this belief cannot be refuted entirely, perhaps you can get a more complete picture of why you forget. Set up a series of imaginary situations to find out why you forget. Your objective will be to see what conditions or situations cause the most forgetting, and then to arrive at some conclusions that will help you understand yourself and the people around you.

Suppose you were to memorize a list of shopping items. Between the time that you memorize the items and the time you wish to recall them, you engage in some activity. If you were to continually repeat the items to yourself until the time when you wish to recall, there would be no forgetting. Normally, however, your activity will not consist of repetition. What if your intervening activity were sleep? How much memory loss or forgetting would occur as compared with if you had been engaged in normal waking activity? The answer: very little. Very little, if any, forgetting occurs during sleep. One hour of wakefulness will cause more loss in recall than eight hours of sleep. When you are awake, you engage in mental activity. This activity causes what is known as interference, and interference is the basic cause of forgetting.

Time alone does not determine the amount of forgetting. What you do between learning and recall is the crucial factor. Sleep between learning and recall causes little or no forgetting. Normal wakefulness does.

The most common form of interference occurs when, between the time when something is learned and the time when it is to be recalled, you think about or learn something else. This is called *retroactive interference*. You learn "A," then learn or think about "B," and then are asked to recall "A." *Pro-active interference* occurs when something one learned inhibits future learning. A secretary who learns to type on one keyboard will find it difficult to proceed to a different type. The fingers will have a tendency to go to the old places. Another instance of pro-active interference occurs when you learn more than one foreign language at a time.

Intensity of interference

You can arrive at some valuable implications for daily living by examining the concept of interference a little more deeply. Using the shopping list as an example once again, compare the interfering effects of two mental activities. Suppose between learning and recall the intervening activity is an easy ride in the car. How would that compare with a drive in heavy traffic? Common sense tells you that the time spent fighting heavy traffic would cause more interference, more forgetting, than an equal amount of time spent in a relaxing drive on the open road. You can arrive at this principle: Forgetting depends, to a large extent, on the intensity of the intervening activity and the degree of tension to which the individual is subjected.

The degree of similarity

The next hypothetical situation is a bit more difficult. Which intervening activity, A or B, would cause more interference between the time you learn the shopping list and the time you wish to recall it: A) doing math problems, or B) learning another shopping list? The answer is that, all other factors being equal, learning another shopping list would cause more forgetting. Another example: Immediately following the learning of a telephone number, what mental act would cause the most forgetting? The answer is: Learning another telephone number. And so, you arrive at another principle: Retention loss varies according to the degree of similarity between the original information you wish to remember and the interjected information or activities.

Experiments have proven how different activities can affect interference. In one experiment, university students were given a list of adjectives to memorize. Between learning and recalling, an activity was interjected. The result was that the number of adjectives recalled varied according to the type of activity to which each student was assigned:

INTERJECTED ACTIVITY	ADJECTIVES RECALLED
reading jokes	45
learning three-digit figures	37
learning nonsense syllables	26
learning adjectives not related to the original ones	22
learning antonyms of the originals	18
learning synonyms of the originals	12

The more similar the interjected material is to the original information, the greater the interference in remembering it.

Implications of the interference theory

Clearly, *the nature* of the intervening or interjected activity does affect how long and how well something is remembered. Keeping that in mind, you may be able to determine whether or not something will be remembered, and also estimate the effort involved in assuring retention. Most people tend to overestimate their ability to remember. You wish to remember something, but are so sure that you will remember that you decide not to jot it down or take special steps to recall it. Thus you end up forgetting the information.

People often reproach themselves for forgetting, when actually they have challenged their memory with a nearly impossible task. The husband who asks his departing wife to stop by the cleaners on her way back home from work, may be asking too much. The mental activity and pressures of a business day can create considerable interference. The same request made before the wife leaves for a relaxing day at the pool may be quite a different matter.

Suppose you meet with an associate to discuss a number of issues. If you are realistic and honest with yourself, you will admit that some of the issues are likely to be forgotten, especially if you know that certain points in the discussion will require intense concentration or emotion. Considering the interference theory, you would do well to deal first with routine matters and save the highly charged or more involving topics for the end. In total, less is likely to be forgotten that way.

You are often called upon to remember numbers or facts. You should ask yourself what type of mental activity you will be engaged in afterward, bearing in mind that the more similar it is to the information, the more likely you are to forget. An unnecessary amount of forgetting occurs during a normal business day precisely because these principles are not taken into account. The secretary who gives her boss some information immediately before he has to attend an important meeting, cannot understand why he later forgets the information. The boss who asks his secretary for some relatively simple information contained in a recent report is surprised at her loss of memory. That the secretary had a few similar reports to deal with may be an explanation.

When You Forget: The Theory of Consolidation

An actual physical difference seems to exist between what may be called long- and short-term memory. Everybody is able to remember remote experiences from his/her childhood, yet may forget something that happened just a day or two ago. It appears that you are likely to forget a recent event. If the event has a special meaning for you, though, or if you recall it for any reason shortly after, you will tend to remember it permanently.

Consider the phenomenon of retrograde amnesia. After a person receives an unusually hard blow upon the head or sustains a traumatic brain injury, he/she may lose consciousness. When the person awakens, he/she is very likely to be unable to recall the events prior to the injury. In recovery, the events furthest preceding the injury are recalled first, and as recovery continues, events closer in time to the accident can gradually be recalled. In many severe cases, those events immediately preceding the accident remain permanently lost.

For events to be stored or "consolidated," into long-term areas, a mental process that requires time appears to be necessary. Electroconvulsive shocks administered across the temples of monkeys a few minutes after they learned a maze produced significant loss of recall, but convulsions induced an hour or more after the learning had little effect. Moreover, the closer in time the shock is administered after the learning trial, the greater is the deterioration of performance in the subsequent test. These and similar observations have been gathered to formulate the theory of consolidation.

"Long-term" and "short-term" memory are relative phrases that have been used by psychologists to simplify understanding of a phenomenon. The brain probably makes no clear-cut distinction. Subjects under hypnosis have been able to recall extremely remote and apparently trivial experiences, experiences we would classify as bearing a short-term function. This suggests the probability that consolidation is a matter of degree. There is no actual sharp dividing line between long- and short-term areas of memory.

The reason the mind discerns between long- and short-term memory can be understood in the following way. Assume someone says, "That man sitting down, the one in the middle, is the father of the girl who is playing the lead role tonight." Without short-term memory, you would forget the subject of the sentence. You would not remember who the person was talking about. Without short-term memory, you would be totally unable to carry on a conversation. You would be unable to remember where you had just placed things and would be unable to keep track of your daily activities. You would, in short, be in a hopeless predicament.

Most memories are short-term and are quickly forgotten. However, it is not necessary to remember everything you have done or seen for every second of the day. The relatively few experiences that have a more significant place in your daily living are stored in long-term memory. Short-term memory acts as a filter system. Thoughts and experiences are held for a period of time while they are evaluated. Most signals are discarded, but those that are special for one reason or another will pass through the system to long-term areas. When the experiences are stored in long-term areas of the brain, they are said to have been *consolidated*. The consolidation process might cause you to forget an event recently experienced. If the event has a special meaning for you, though, or if you recall the event shortly afterward, you will tend to remember it permanently.

Most forgetting is done shortly after learning. Items such as phone numbers, dates, names, and isolated facts may be forgotten in seconds, unless the item is included in your thoughts shortly afterward.

Implications of consolidation theory

Obviously, there are implications here, particularly for business or social situations where the learning of facts or dates may be followed by unrelated mental activity. In many instances, *forgetting can be avoided by a simple, quick review before going on to some other mental activity.* The best time to review is immediately or shortly after learning. In learning a large body of organized material, however, it may be good to review an hour or so afterward. This is because some experiments have shown that more material was recalled an hour after the lecture, than immediately afterward.

This phenomenon may be explained by the Serial Position effect which shows that after learning any list or body of information, memory will be better for the first and last items you learn. Immediately after hearing a lecture, reading a chapter, or learning any sequence of ideas, you tend to remember most clearly the beginning and the end. After an hour or so, however, you are more apt to view the material as a whole, seeing more of the main ideas, as opposed to details that happened to be at the beginning or end. Therefore, in the case of long assignments or lectures, it is helpful to relax for a short while before reviewing.

the art of recall

Recall bears a directly proportional relationship to learning. If information has been correctly processed and committed to memory, you will recall it. Therefore, if you heed and practice the suggestions in the first two parts of this book, your memory will dramatically improve. Many instances occur, nevertheless, when material is learned but recall does not produce all that the learning process has taken in. It is rare to experience more annoyance and frustration than when you "know" the past but cannot recall it. Have you ever left an essay examination feeling somewhat uneasy and wishing to discuss the test with someone? Upon doing so, you may realize that you omitted an entire topic of central importance.

You probably feel like banging your head against the wall when something you were unable to remember yesterday comes back to you with notorious clarity today—after you no longer have the need to recall it. You have countless memories. Sometimes events from long ago come back, and for apparently little reason. But to sort out just the right memory from the massive accumulations at the precise time and place that you wish, is often quite a feat.

Our mental activities are extremely complicated. No machine can be built that would remember how to play baseball with the precision and accuracy of average players. Though startling advances in technology have made possible the guidance of missiles and rockets (these machines are run by a computer which has been furnished with an electronic "memory" for the entire course), far more miraculous is the guidance system involved in the judgement of a fly ball by an outfielder. No instrument will ever come close to matching an average human being in his/her number of memories and the ability to process them in unconscious and conscious behavior. The brain can be regarded as one mighty super-computer. It receives data, stores certain inputs, and recalls and processes information just the way a computer does. And, as in the case of a machine, a disturbance of one component may cause malfunctioning of the entire process.

Interference

It is well accepted that the mind can process only one signal at a time. Malfunctions in recall take place when other signals interfere with the recall process. The businessman tries to remember what he wished to say in a letter, but is still bothered by the argument he had a few minutes ago. The student, instead of concentrating completely on the problem, may worry about what will happen if she fails, what her parents will say, etc. She may be notified that only ten minutes remain and that she must rush in order to finish. Signals screaming "hurry, think fast," cram the brain. Obviously these are not ideal conditions for recall.

Unconscious factors affecting mental blanks

The mental blank during a testing situation exemplifies one of the extremest forms of recall malfunction. The examinee suddenly is unable to recall even the most elementary concepts in a subject for a period of time. The duration of the blank may vary from twenty seconds to many minutes. Once the test is finished, however, recall is back to normal.

The dynamics of the unconscious may play a part in causing mental blanks. Sigmund Freud was the first man to succeed in convincing people that behavior is determined by more than conscious thought. A great many things that we do are due to the activity of our unconscious minds. We are unaware of its activity but the unconscious mind accounts for the fact that no two people think and behave alike. At first, Freud was scoffed at by his contemporaries, but today few psychologists would deny that the unconscious exerts an extremely powerful influence on what we remember, how we remember, and consequently how we react to certain situations.

Your attempts to recall most often will not be hindered by the dynamics of your unconscious mind, but occasionally obstructions do occur. Whether or not obstruction does occur depends to a large extent on how you approach a stressful situation. If you approach a test feeling confident in yourself and in your knowledge, you will not experience an obstruction to memory. On the other hand, lack of confidence in yourself and your abilities, plus a fear of failure and consequent humiliation, may contribute to poor recall.

Your mental state

Intense mental activity increases interference and makes forgetting more likely to occur later on. Tension and excitement are also powerful factors in forgetting, if they are present at the exact time of recall. Yet frequently people do not modify their learning habits to take this factor into account. Usually an individual spends the same amount of time in preparing material, whether it be for a lecture or for a debate. Should he/she prepare better for the former or the latter? The debate or argument would obviously require more preparation. It is a matter of asking yourself, "What will be my mental state at the time when I will be expected to recall this information? What will the situation be? Will the conditions be formal or informal? Will my audience be friendly or hostile?" The previous questions and similar ones can help determine the tension level of the recall situation and you can then take more precise steps.

A young man in his early twenties told me of his not-so-unusual problem. It seemed that often he would be in the close company of a lovely young lady, the lights would be lowered, and he would say something to fit the occasion, such as, "Oh, I'm really crazy about you . . . uh . . . honey." A total blank would set in. It was understandable considering the excitement of the recall situation. I told him to prepare for this situation by reviewing the name of a certain young woman more thoroughly than others. The degree of preparation should depend upon your assessment of the recall situation.

How to Recall

If you were asked to name the ninth President of the United States, you would hope the answer would be retrieved instantly. If the answer does not come right away, you may repeat "ninth President, ninth President," over and over again, hoping that somehow the answer will return. Often, by simply repeating the question to yourself, the answer may be recalled, but there are better ways.

How often has this happened to you? You wanted to recall something but could not. Then, long after you have given up, by chance you think of some object or event related to that which you wished to remember, and all of a sudden your answer is recalled. Tension may have caused your main path of recall to be blocked when you made the conscious effort to recall, but accidentally, in the process of thinking, you later took an *alternate path* of recall. You do not have to wait for these haphazard recollections to occur. This chapter shows how you can make recall come by design.

The spectrum of recall

Information may be located in one or many areas of the brain. Memory for visions will be located in one area, memory for words in another, your own thoughts on a subject in still another area, and so on. If you have used the techniques of discrimination and association, you will have the starting points for recall. However, in some instances, you may not have applied those techniques. Nevertheless, you may still touch upon a starting point.

Following are a number of suggestions that describe the means by which you can scan the mind and retrieve information when memory fails. All of the suggestions discuss different ways of thinking. Thinking has often been called "inner communication." When you think, you send signals through your brain, which elicit knowledge and experiences.

Think of everything

Information is located in the brain cells. It is the task of memory to use all the avenues of approach possible to the various areas of the brain in order to draw out the desired information. Take the instance of a young girl who leaves her house for school in the morning, taking her umbrella along because it is raining. That evening she returns home for dinner, at which time her mother mentions a musical she had heard by a man named Jacques Brel. The girl suddenly drops her spoon, jumps up, and rushes to open the door. Sure enough, the umbrella is missing and she sadly concludes that she forgot it somewhere.

"You must try to remember where it is," says the mother. "Remember all the places you were today. Then, for each place, try to remember whether or not you had the umbrella. Think of every time you put the umbrella down, and afterwards whether or not you picked it up. Try to visualize yourself and see whether or not you had the umbrella at certain times. Eventually, you should be able to have a reasonably good idea of where you left it."

In other words, she must not give up. As long as she keeps her thoughts actively on the subject, she has a chance to strike upon some memory that will give her the answer. Similarly, if you forget a name for the moment, do not give up. Keep the mind moving. Think of everything relating to the person. Ask yourself if you remember his wife's name and perhaps while thinking of her name, his will be retrieved. If that doesn't work, think of what he does for a living, or think of your last conversation with him. Anything might serve as a trigger for recall.

Classify thoughts

A mental activity that will surely recall knowledge is the classification of thoughts. If you were asked to tell a joke right at this moment, you might have trouble recalling even one. However, if you were to use the method of classification, recall would be no problem. You could search your memory for the first category—possibly husband/wife jokes. Next you might think of doctor jokes or ethnic stories, and probably several would be recalled in each category.

A student in a class of art history is shown a painting and asked to name the artist. She thinks for a moment, but cannot come up with the correct answer. There is, however, no reason to give up at that point. The key to unlocking the knowledge from the depths of her mind lies in organizing her knowledge on the subject. She should look at the painting and try to classify it in some way. Perhaps she classifies it by the style or period. She may decide that the style is impressionistic. In that case, she tries to recall all the impressionist painters that she knows and in so doing may come upon the name she has forgotten. If this fails, she may decide that the painting belongs to the Renaissance period and once again goes down the list. By classifying thoughts in this way, new avenues of transmission are opened to release knowledge.

Categorizing can be especially effective in remembering names. If you have forgotten a name, you could think of the face and ask yourself if the name starts with the letter A. Then try B, and so on. When you get to J, you may believe the name starts with that letter. Then try a few names beginning with J, for example, Jane, Janice, etc., and suddenly the name will be recalled. Categorizing may be a slow method of recall, but it frequently works when all else fails.

How often have you had the feeling of having forgotten to do a chore, yet no matter how hard you try to remember it, you just can't? Recall can be achieved by asking yourself questions such as "Could it be anything to do with the job?" You then search your mind for all aspects of the job situation and if you have indeed forgotten some chore pertaining to the job, some aspect you scan having a relationship to the chore will help you remember. If the job category does not turn up anything, you can then ask yourself if it pertains to the family, or social affairs, or materials and possessions. These categories can be mentally subdivided into further compartments. After deciding to search the "family" compartment, you can then ask yourself if it has anything to do with the husband, then the kids and parents. Materials and possessions may be broken down to the car, the house, clothes, and so on. When each category is *isolated* by the mind for a few brief but powerful seconds, correct recall will almost always occur.

State-dependent recall

You are surely familiar with the experience of traveling and being lost or unsure of the proper way. You then come to some familiar place that you recognize as being on the way to your destination. At that moment, you are no longer lost and are able to remember the rest of the way. This is an example of the phenomenon called *state-dependent recall*, meaning that recall takes place best when the environment is most similar to the environment in which the information was originally learned. Experiments working with and testing students have confirmed this phenomenon. Students tested in the same classroom, at the same time of day, and in the same seat as when the original learning took place, scored higher than a group tested under different conditions.

This presents some interesting implications for recall. The most important is that when the recall situation is different from the learning situation, the advantage need not be lost. Your mind can reconstruct the original environment. Suppose you are confronted with a test question, the answer to which escapes you at first. You may try to reproduce the original learning environment as closely as possible. Then other recollections will follow.

The act of reproducing the original learning situation is extremely effective under conditions of severe tension, because the *visual reproductions are far less likely to be "blocked."* If ever you find yourself in a "mental blank," you can snap yourself out of it by referring to a visual picture of the original learning environment.

Recall your own thoughts

The advantages obtained by contributing your own knowledge of a subject while learning have been stressed. This method of learning keeps your mind occupied, aids comprehension, and helps in organizing your knowledge and judging the value of ideas. You tend to remember your own thoughts better than those of someone else. Whenever you interject your own thoughts on a subject, an association is formed consisting of your own ideas and opinions and any new knowledge. For example, if you can remember being critical of an author or speaker, it is then easy to remember *why* you were critical, and certain points that were made can be recalled. Naturally, the more thoughts you had while learning was taking place, the more paths you will have available for recall.

Recalling your own thoughts to remember reading material can be accomplished systematically. The surest method is to draw upon the purposes you had in mind while learning. For example, if you are questioned about the contents of an article called "Victims of a Curse," ask yourself, "What would have been my purpose in reading such a title?" You could then state that your purposes were to find out what the curse consisted of, who the victims were, and why they were cursed. This gives you a starting point for recalling your thoughts. If you indeed did formulate these thoughts while learning, they will return to you as your mind focuses on these questions.

Think about the article on the energy crisis entitled "The Need for Balance." Do some thoughts come to mind? Did you agree with the author? What were your anticipations when you skimmed the article? Did the author say what you expected? Turn now only to the questions on page 72. Answer the questions without rereading the article.

When all attempts are exhausted

If, after you have reorganized your knowledge, drawn your own thoughts, recreated the original learning environment, and thought of anything related to the subject, you still cannot recall, there is one last hope. You simply pack the problem into the unconscious mind and wait for a more opportune moment, when nervousness, irritability, or whatever, are not present. Perhaps the recollection will come back when you least expect it. You can facilitate this possibility by firmly stating your intention to remember. You may vocalize in this manner: "I know that I know Betty's birthday. I want to recall it. I will recall it." Say it loud, clear, and with plenty of sincerity, then relax and think of something else, and the brain will respond to the sound of your voice in due time.

You can speed up the process by talking to others about some subject that contains information you have forgotten. If you have forgotten the name of the person starring in a certain motion picture, talk about various aspects of the picture for awhile. Your unconscious mind will be ready and alert to recognize a thought that will trigger memory.

The ability to recall can be improved. Here are a couple of exercises which require you to get the various parts of the brain communicating.

RECALL EXERCISE #1

At the end of a day, try to recall everything you did that day. Recall, for the most part, by visualizing. Your final product should be a chronological recap of the day. However, recollections can come in any order. That is as it should be. One activity will recall others.

RECALL EXERCISE #2

Try to do the same for an entire year. If you record everything you remember as you go along, you will be amazed at how much you can remember. It may take several days to record an impressive array of recollections, but you may find it quite interesting. It will also give you a good idea of how the recall process works.

RECALL EXERCISE #3

This game can be a lot of fun. List the letters of the alphabet in order. Then have someone call out a sentence. Some famous statement will do fine. Underneath each letter of the alphabet, write the corresponding letters of the sentence as illustrated:

```
A  B  C  D  E  F  G  H  I  J  K  L  M  N  O  P  Q  R  S  T  U  V  W  X  Y  Z
D  A  M  N  T  H  E  T  O  R  P  E  D  O  E  S  F  U  L  L  S  P  E  E  D  A
```

You are to treat the resultant pairs of letters as the initials of famous people. Your objective is to be able to recall the names of these famous people. For the first set of initials, you may come up with the composer, Anton Dvorák. For the second, you might choose the American Revolutionary general and traitor, Benedict Arnold, and the third might be the author, Carson McCullers. *This game should be played competitively and it should be timed.* That will stimulate pressure. In other words, the person or couple that can think of the most names in a given period, say 10 minutes, wins. The technique here is to keep the mind active. Keep trying names to yourself. Never let the mind go blank. This game is exciting, challenging, good practice—and fun.

RECALL EXERCISE #4

This is the very well known "Concentration" game. An ordinary deck of playing cards is spread face down on a table. Two or three players each turn over two cards. The player who turns over the two matching cards (matching in number—not in suit) gets to put that pair in his pile. The player who has the largest pile at the end wins. The key here is to remember the location of cards that were turned over. Children, even at age five, can compete with adults at this game because they naturally visualize.

Introducing Part IV

The study of concentration improvement, in particular, cannot be separated from the study of personality development. You have seen how to enhance concentration by using specific techniques with printed matter. However, if someone has just been deeply affected by another's insulting remark, it may still be quite impossible to concentrate while reading or listening.

You notice the problem of concentration when you try to read and you become distracted. The habit of mind-wandering may have developed because for years you let your mind wander on easy, everyday tasks. The following section shows how other branches of psychology contribute to, and draw from, this study of memory. If you use the principles, with modifications, in other fields, you will be more likely to concentrate and remember.

part IV

memory and practical psychology

CHAPTER 14

concentration in everyday life

A man called Peter is working at his job. He is not working very efficiently, however. He is not working at a pace and with the alertness necessary for him to advance in his field. Peter would like to be more productive but he finds that his mind wanders quite often. Today many of his thoughts are about his 10-year-old boy who is having trouble in school. Later, at dinner, he engages in some conversation—a conversation that is really the product of two wandering minds.

After dinner the boy asks Peter if he would help with the homework, and Peter accepts. Within two minutes, though, something happens. The boy looks at his father and senses that his mind is somewhere else. Where is his mind now? You may have guessed it! His mind is now on problems with his job. His thoughts are then interrupted by his wife who suggests that they go away to relax for the weekend. No way! It may sound paradoxical, but the person who characteristically cannot concentrate, will also have difficulty relaxing and enjoying himself.

But this is all ridiculous. Do you realize that with the same amount of mental effort, Peter could be successful at his job, relate better to his child's problems, enjoy his weekends and vacation, and in fact, be successful at just about any endeavor that he engages in? It takes no more effort to succeed than it does to fail. The only skill necessary is to stay mentally "with it"—to give complete attention to the right thing at the right time.

Does Peter remind you of anyone? If you are honest, then you must realize that to some extent at least, Peter reminds you of yourself. We are all plagued, though to varying degrees, with the phenomenon of mind-wandering, no matter what our age, race, sex, or position in life. We can all benefit by learning a little about why our minds wander, and how we can take steps to reduce the occurrence of this wasteful activity.

How Concentration Affects Some Problems of Everyday Life

The mental blank

As a beginning example, consider the high school student who is taking an examination. He has prepared for the test —perhaps not as well as he could have, but he should be able to give a decent account of himself. Then a couple of tough questions appear consecutively, and suddenly, he totally loses his ability to think clearly. At times during the test he forgets even the most elementary concepts of the course. Later he may describe the experience as having a "mental blank."

Was it really a mental blank? Perhaps "mental congestion" would be a better term. He probably was thinking of too many things—things which had no business entering his mind at that particular time. He was, most likely, thinking of what could happen if he failed, what his folks would say, what his friends would think, the fact that his friends would all be in college and he would be the one not to make it, and so on. The problem was that he was not thinking of the right things at the right time.

Speech making

The problem of memory you may encounter in giving a speech is quite similar to the "mental blank" in an examination. All you have to do is to start thinking about what the audience may think if you forget your lines, and you surely will be in trouble. The brain has often been likened to a mighty computer. If too many signals enter the mind, with each signal going to a different section of the brain, the computer "jams," and no signals are processed.

Sales

People who work on commission, such as salespeople, are often more affected by attention lapses than the average person. Why? Because the salesperson in the midst of an interview will often find him/herself thinking thoughts like, "I wonder if he is going to buy or not. Gee, if he takes the large order, that will mean X number of dollars in my pocket." These thoughts prevent the salesperson from giving his/her full attention to the unique problems of the prospect, and the finer points of sales.

Overeating

The inability to lose weight has been explained by psychologists and medical doctors in a variety of ways. No doubt the reasons are complex, but at the heart of the problem of eating more than what is good for one's body, lies the matter of concentration.

People can eat without thinking about it. The person who overeats habitually does not give attention to the food he/she is eating, and consequently he/she eats too much. If you are heavier than you would like to be, then into which of the following categories do you fit? Are you the television watcher who anxiously awaits the next turn of events while busily munching? Or are you normally engaged in table chatter while eating? Do you go out to eat a delicious meal and become so preoccupied with other matters that you can hardly remember afterward how it tasted? If no conversation is available, do you use mealtime to catch up on your reading?

If you want to lose weight, the first thing you must start doing immediately is make a sustained effort to give full attention to the pleasures of eating, and enjoy your food. That's exactly right! The overweight person, contrary to popular belief, does not enjoy food because he/she is too busy thinking of other things. If you decide to think about your food while eating, if you let yourself savor *every single bite*, you will find that your body will require less of whatever you are eating at the time. Meals will also become considerably more pleasurable. But this would seem to cause more harm than good. If you learn to enjoy eating, wouldn't you tend to eat more, not less? No, not really. Eating ceases to be pleasurable when the mind senses that you have had enough. Concentration makes the mind realize more quickly that you have had your fill.

Stress

An individual under great stress will usually find it more difficult to keep his/her mind on a particular thing. Even occurrences that are unrelated to the cause of the worry or concern can disrupt the desired trend of thought. Yet you have probably seen how some successful people can consistently get into tense situations and still concentrate quite well on whatever they happen to be engaged in. It is not the amount of stress or excitement in your day that is the major factor in concentration, but rather the manner in which you deal with the stressful situation. If you get used to dealing with problems efficiently, as they arise, you will be exercising good habits as far as the issue of concentration is concerned. Distractions are far more likely to occur, though, if after being confronted with a stressful situation, you *do not* cope with the problem. Someone may avoid serious problems by saying things such as "Please, I don't want to think about that now," or "I'll do it tomorrow." Procrastination, stagnation, and avoiding decisions all keep problems from consciousness for a while, but these actions do not really alleviate stress. As long as the stressful situation remains, and it is not dealt with, the problem will play a part in your behavior.

When you are in a tense situation, chemicals are secreted by those brain cells that would be active in dealing with the particular problem. These chemicals serve to facilitate mental activity. If you cope with a stressful condition, these chemicals are used in a healthy way. If, however, you do not cope, but procrastinate or avoid the problem, the chemicals do not disappear. They remain in the brain and cause a condition of general excitability and distraction. These chemicals can cause distractions even though you do not give the worry conscious attention.

One implication, then, for improving concentration, is to deal with anything that may be bothering you and get it out of the way. Some problems cannot be resolved because you are powerless to deal with them. We all relive worries about things that happened in the past or about things that are beyond our control. Dale Carnegie once said that "90 percent of the things we worry about never happen, and the other 10 percent will happen anyway." Perhaps Mr. Carnegie exaggerated in his figures, yet the point is quite clear. Many things are not worth worrying about.

Often people do not know what is bothering them. They have a feeling of turmoil in their stomachs, and are severely distractible but they cannot identify the exact worry, fear, or problem that is causing the discomfort. This condition is worse, and will cause more distraction, than if the cause of the worry is known. Whenever you get the feeling, then, that something is bothering you, you must take steps to assure that the problem does not impair your concentration in your job or other activities. At times the fear or problem may not surface immediately. You must then draw it out by using mental classification. Isolate certain categories which most problems tend to stem from. Ask yourself if the trouble has anything to do with your job, and consider that category of life for a moment. If all is okay there, you may ask if it has anything to do with your family, your love life, or just about anything. If you think only of a certain category for a moment, the problem will surface if it falls into that category.

Quite often when you attempt to draw out problems in this manner, you will discover a number of things that may have been bothering you. Fine. A good procedure, then, would be to make a list of all the reasons you may have for being tense or nervous. After you have compiled a number of problems, then evaluate each one from the standpoint of whether or not you have any control over the matter. For each one that you judge as uncontrollable—that is, the situation is a thing of the past, or may or may not happen no matter what you do—draw a thick black line through it. As you do that, vow that you will no longer let the thought bother you. There is a reciprocity between the body and the mind. The mind remembers ritualistic actions. You will tend to push aside these concerns and in so doing pave the way for clearer thought and concentrated action. For those items that can be resolved you must decide on courses of action, and then act without hesitation.

Goals and plans

Did Peter, mentioned earlier, ever concentrate on his job for long? Yes, he did once. The boss had approached him and said sternly, "You had better get this project finished by tomorrow or look for another job." He worked at maximum effectiveness and made the deadline. Immediately afterward, he returned to his usual, barely acceptable performance. Peter was able to pay attention to his work at that time because he had a goal to complete the project at a given time—and because he was motivated by fear.

If we are motivated by fear we will normally concentrate. The trouble with most people is that they cease being motivated once the threat is no longer in existence. The motive of fear will be replaced by the longer-lasting motive of pride and accomplishment if a human being perceives him/herself as gradually attaining a worthwhile long-range goal. The act of formulating goals in life enhances concentration on tasks that relate to the goal. The first implication, then, is to set goals in life. You must ask yourself, basically, what you want. You must decide what would constitute success for you. Most people do not have a clear idea of what they want in life and as a result their minds wander aimlessly from one thought to another. A good way to set goals is to force yourself to describe a typical day in your life as you would like it to be five years from now and write down your description. From this description you should also derive the skills, character traits, or knowledge that you would need to attain your goals. Acquiring the skills and traits will thereafter be approached with increased concentration.

Next, write out a detailed plan describing the step-by-step path toward the attainment of your ultimate goal. Planning helps you become organized, and personal organization aids concentration and efficiency. Planning also helps you set short-range goals and see steps along the way.

meditation: an exercise in concentration and relaxation

What meditation is

Meditation is the act of prolonged concentration on one particular thought or object. The object could consist of anything. If you are practicing the concentration exercises suggested in the previous chapter, then you have already meditated. If you have given total concentration to just fresh air or food, then it may be stated that you meditated on these things.

Meditation is also an exercise in relaxation. In actuality, the abilities to relax and to concentrate are closely related. One must be able to relax in order to concentrate and vice versa. The two abilities have a reciprocal relationship. Any exercise that helps one will help the other. Meditation will be a continuation of the practice exercises in concentration discussed in the previous chapter. You will be more likely to concentrate on daily activities if you practice meditation regularly.

MEDITATION EXERCISE #1:
A GROUP EXERCISE

It is easier to give full concentration if you have a voice to listen to. Therefore, one member of the group should act as leader. The participants should give total attention to the directions of the leader. The room should be quiet. Participants should be seated upright but comfortably. Your hands should rest flat on a clean desk, or on your lap. The exact position is not essential, but you should take a motionless position for a period of 20 to 25 minutes without losing circulation. The instructions can vary but below is one method that beginners will find easy to focus upon. The leader should speak slowly, with long pauses between instructions. The entire exercise should last about 20-25 minutes. The leader reads the following directions:
1. Close your eyes. Wiggle the neck, shoulders, and arms for a few seconds. Get physically loose!

2. Keeping the eyes closed, imagine that you and your chair are suspended in space. As you lean back, the chair starts to drift backward. You are floating and drifting backward.

3. You are drifting backward and downward into a long, dark tunnel. Only you exist in this tunnel—nothing else. It is very peaceful. The air is fresh and clean. You are still drifting downward and backward, deeper into the tunnel. (Emphasize the peaceful atmosphere, the floating, drifting, etc.).

4. Gradually you come to a stop. In the distance, at the mouth of the tunnel, you see a candle. Really visualize that candle. See the flame . . . the aura . . . see it in vivid color . . . make your vision as clear as possible. Work on that image for a few moments.

5. The candle starts to drift closer . . . and you know that as this candle hovers over an area of your body, that area will become totally relaxed. All muscular and nervous activity will cease completely from that portion of the body.

6. The candle drifts toward the feet. It is hovering about a foot above the toes. Feel the warmth. All activity ceases in the toes—and now in the feet, so that the feet, with full weight, are allowed to fall where they may. The candle drifts higher . . . to the ankles . . . to the legs . . . all activity ceases . . . You feel totally relaxed and free of tension. (Continue in this manner until all areas of the body have been covered. Include the relaxing of facial muscles, i.e., the chin, tongue, eyes, and forehead.)

7. Now your entire body is completely at rest. See your body as if you were outside yourself. See every portion of your body in a state of total peace and calm. Relax every portion of your body. The candle is hovering about a foot above your forehead. You know that this candle can take you on a beautiful and glorious adventure. Assume now an air of exhilarated anticipation.

    You feel a force coming from deep within your body, reaching out and taking hold of the candle—effortlessly yet tightly. The candle now starts to rise. And you feel yourself leaving your body. You are in spirit form, and you feel so light and free.

8. The candle rises higher and you feel yourself rising with it. You are floating higher and higher. Soon you will be leaving the tunnel. It is a beautiful, clear, soft summer night outside. You are outside now. Feel that soft, beautiful summer breeze. See the candle. There are clouds up above and stars high in the sky. It is so beautiful. You are floating higher with every breath of that clean, fresh air. And you can float in any shape or position—right side up, upside down—any conceivable way.

9. Continue on through the clouds and up to the stars. Keep reinforcing the image of the candle, the air, the scenery, the relaxed and beautiful feelings, etc.

10. Now you are approaching the highest star, the top of the universe. You float to it and lie down and stretch out. You can do this because the star is your own creation. (Once again, remind participants to see and feel everything.)

11. The sun now starts to come out and lovely, peaceful scenery unfolds. You see pretty pastures, trees, etc., and a clear pond with flowers surrounding it. See it all in vivid color. You want to swim in the pond . . . so the candle starts to take you down. Once again, you are just floating, (use words like easily, tumbling, etc.).

12. Describe the experience of entering into and floating on the water. See and feel all details.

13. The candle now starts to take you back to the tunnel. You are re-entering the tunnel and drifting downward. You feel so good, and as you re-enter your body you bring that feeling with you. You have re-entered the body. You let go of the candle. The candle starts to rise. It is leaving the tunnel. Take one last good look at the candle. Now it is gone.

14. You feel yourself rising slowly. You are leaving the tunnel. You are returning to this room. Now open your eyes and wake up.

After you have finished this exercise, ask yourself how long it took. When you subsequently look at the clock, you might be quite surprised at the way time passed. This is a common perception when you are visualizing and concentrating. You should also feel nice and relaxed.

MEDITATION EXERCISE #2:
AN INDIVIDUAL EXERCISE

You can concentrate on and imagine anything you wish, and if the contents of your visions are pleasant and peaceful, your body will become more relaxed. If you meditate regularly, you will become more relaxed in normal waking life as well. It will not always be possible, however, to have a voice to focus upon, so you may want to try an individual exercise. Although more difficult, it can be done with practice.

Listen to soft music (preferably instrumental). Concentrate on the music, and imagine your entire self floating in space and in a sort of rhythm with the music. You may add scenery. Try imagining the ocean or shore, with the waves also. Actually, a great many visions will suffice. Experiment and determine what visions and sounds are easiest to focus upon.

Meditation to aid recall

Problems in recall can arise under conditions of frustration, tension, and pressure, as mentioned earlier. You can use the relaxation exercise as an aid to recall. First, you should be alone. State your intention to remember, in a clear, complete sentence, such as "I am going to remember where I placed . . ." (Be sure to say it aloud.)

Next, go into the meditation exercise. When you are completely in a state of enjoyable relaxation, turn your attention to the object, person, place, or subject in question. Visualize it, and allow your mind to recall anything you know about the subject. All the while remain completely relaxed. You may note your mind recalling other facts associated with the subject, but not the particular fact you wish to remember. That is O.K. Just keep the mind going in a state of relaxed concentration. Be patient! Do not hurry. Bear in mind that your overall objective is relaxation. Recall must be considered incidental. Take that casual frame of mind, and the desired recall will come eventually.

Preface to Chapter 16

Many people in this day and age have an aversion to technical material. This is an unfortunate situation, since many interesting careers are missed unnecessarily, and a great wealth of fascinating information is avoided, because many individuals take one look at a technical chapter and turn it away without giving themselves a chance. Often scientific material is not as difficult to concentrate on and retain as it would seem, if you apply the reading techniques mentioned in Chapter 7.

Try to formulate your approach structure as quickly as possible. Decide how you would want to recall this chapter of *Memory Power* for the benefit of an audience. The second paragraph in the chapter should give you a logical pattern. You could see your first objective as: being able to state how information gets from the environment to the brain, then to state how the memories are retained, and then to state how the information is recalled. Think how you would phrase your first sentence. In any biological chapter, it may be easy to get bogged down in scientific terms and names of chemicals. Do not worry! Read only to fulfill your purposes and you will naturally fall into an organized order of priorities.

CHAPTER 16

the physiological
aspects of memory

This chapter contains no techniques that will improve your ability to remember or concentrate, just as learning about the mechanics of an automobile will not improve your driving. Nevertheless, if you have fully digested the ideas and principles in the preceding chapters and, hopefully, if you are applying some of these principles to your own life, you have a good knowledge of how the mind functions from a practical standpoint. Yet no one can ever truly be knowledgeable on any subject unless they have some idea of *why* some methods, suggestions, or procedures work. When you see the reason behind performing a certain action, you are more likely to perform that action. This chapter will furnish further insight and knowledge about the human mind.

The action of memory is essentially threefold: First, the brain must receive information about the environment. Second, it must store or retain that information in some form over a passage of time. And last, it must be possible to gain access to that information when needed.

Where Is Memory Located?

The nervous system has the capability to transmit memories to cells within the brain, where they can be stored in some way. Many scientists believe that everything experienced or learned produces some physical change in the brain. Where do these signals go, and where are they stored when they are not present in our consciousness?

The cerebral cortex, the outer layer of the brain, is the structure generally identified as being concerned with recognition of objects and symbols, thought, learning, and memory. Studies in evolution have shown that the cerebral cortex becomes larger and has more convolutions (folds) relative to the rest of the nervous system, as one ascends the evolutionary ladder. The mouse has a more highly developed cortex than most fish, the monkey higher than the mouse, and man higher than the monkey. Size and weight of the brain is not the key factor. The cat does not have a larger cortex than the alligator, yet the *relative* size of the cortex compared with the rest of its body is higher in the cat than the alligator, indicating that the former is the more intelligent animal.

A recent study showed that the cortex can enlarge and develop depending upon the activities and environment of an organism. Young rats were divided into two groups. The first group was raised in an enriched environment, being taught a number of tricks. The second group was raised in an unstimulating, impoverished environment. The stimulated rats were found, after a period of several months, to have demonstrated superiority in learning ability. Later examination revealed a sizeable difference in weight of the cortex in favor of the stimulated rats.

Continued experimentation focused on determining a more exact location of function. Stimulation of a certain area between the parietal and temporal lobes, in conscious patients undergoing brain surgery, created vivid, complex memories. A girl who had a portion of her skull removed in the course of an operation said that when a certain area was touched by a needle, she heard familiar music so clearly that she believed a phonograph had been turned on nearby. Stimulation of other areas revealed other experiences that were recognizable memories. Memory for language appears to lie in the dominant hemisphere of the cortex (i.e., the left side for right-handed people, the right for left-handed). Damage to this particular area leads to a condition known as aphasia, which is characterized by an inability to understand the written or spoken word.

Despite this seemingly convincing evidence supporting the localization theory, valid objections can be raised to it. The most forceful is that if a certain brain tissue known to be essential to remembering a response, is cut, the result will be that although the animal forgets the response, it will take fewer trials to relearn it. "Saving" has taken place. (*Saving* occurs when, after having learned something which is later forgotten, you can relearn it in a shorter time than was needed when it was learned originally.) This suggests that some memory existed elsewhere and that this other area was able to assume these functions. It seems justifiable to conclude that data is routed through the nerve tracts to certain places on the cortex where similar knowledge and experiences are stored. However, traces of these experiences are also routed to more than one cell and to various locations. Memories of visual experiences are routed to certain areas; memories of hearing, touch, and smell to still others. Therefore, storage for a single experience may be located in a number of cells at various positions on the cortex.

Any experience is composed of a number of visual, verbal, and tactile or kinesthetic memories. Throughout the brain, there are innumerable interconnections and passageways that serve to tie these memories together so that the recalling of one memory can trigger the recollection of an entire experience. Events can be recalled by hearing a sound, seeing a site again, or feeling something familiar. By hearing, seeing, or feeling only one small part of an event, the entire event can be recalled through the use of these interconnections.

It holds true, then, that the more areas of the brain that you utilize to store an experience, the more easily you will recall it. This hypothesis is behind the suggestions to store knowledge using as many mental faculties as possible. In recall, if only a single area can be tapped, it will start a chain reaction bringing forth memories from other areas of the brain. By using as many areas as possible, you will have alternative paths for recall should the primary path be blocked due to nervousness or distraction.

Right and left brains

One of the most intriguing developments of modern research has been the discovery that our brains are comprised of two hemispheres which look almost symmetrical and identical (the left side is usually a little larger). They each are concerned with a separate set of functions.

When it comes to processing simple sensory and motor tasks, the division of labor is clear-cut. The left side of the brain controls the right side of the body, and the right side of the brain controls the left side of the body. Thus, the right hemisphere receives signals from the left eye and vice versa. When mental tasks become more complex, however, so does the division of responsibility. The left side is active when you are thinking and using words, computing, organizing thoughts, and reasoning logically. The right side is concerned with the recognition and construction of forms. It is involved with music, intuition, and creativity.

The right side has more mystique. Most of us would like to think of ourselves as being right-brain oriented or dominant. Yet bear in mind that it is the left side that communicates with the outside world. An architect may conceive of a beautiful design with her right hemisphere, but without the left, she could not remember the essential numbers and words to put her creation into effect.

The two hemispheres must communicate with each other for many tasks of memory. A facial form is recognized by the right hemisphere. The signals must then be sent to the left, which interprets the signals and recalls the sounds that comprise the name. If the nerve fiber connecting the two hemispheres is cut (such surgery has been used to successfully relieve people suffering from severe epilepsy), the people show a distinct inability to recognize faces and forms, though they can function normally in many respects.

138

Numerous experiments have been conducted with these people. The procedures usually entail presenting one side of the brain with a task of memory by covering one eye. For example, a spoon is held up as the right eye is covered. Hence, the information goes to the right hemisphere. (Remember that the left eye goes to the right side.) When later asked what was presented, the person will state that he/she has forgotten. When a fork, cigarette, and spoon are all held up, and the subject is asked to make a choice, the subject is more amazed than anyone else as his/her left hand (the side controlled by the right brain) spontaneously points to the spoon.

Despite the fact that the right brain has retained the information, the left brain describes the experience as forgetting. Unless experiences can be stored in the language area, the brain will have a difficult time recalling. Possibly the reason that experiences cannot be recalled until about age four or so is because the left side is not developed and does not organize the data. Yet the brain does store experiences from early childhood in an intuitive, nonverbal way. As psychoanalysis has shown, these early impressions have a profound influence on our emotional development.

It is in the area of emotions that the right brain has power. Visual information can be presented to the right brain which can cause laughter or rage. When information is presented to the left side of these split-brain subjects (information that is retained by the right), frowning and wincing may occur as the left brain gives the wrong answers.

Implication

Very often we receive information and get a gut feeling that we understand and could recall when we wish. How often have you comfortably believed that you will remember what to say when the time comes? Your right brain, connecting to your emotional area, can give you this false feeling of satisfaction. Yet when the recall situation arrives, the words just do not come out right—if they come at all. You must take steps to make the connection complete. If information is to be communicated, you must make sure to organize the information in a logical verbal construction. Until you do that, you cannot say you will remember.

How Data Is Transmitted

Data is transmitted through the environment by light rays, sound waves, and by degrees of pressure detected by your sense of touch. Obviously, the brain cannot deal with all of these different types of "input" in their original form. These signals must be converted into a form that the nervous system can understand.

The actual process by which the brain, in conjunction with the senses, converts the rays and waves received from the environment is beyond the scope of this book. Suffice it to say that all data transmitted by the nervous system is converted into a form of electrical energy. These electrical impulses are transmitted to various parts of the nervous system, as well as the brain, along a special type of cell called a neuron (Fig. 1). The electrical impulses transmitted by the neurons are representative of the input rays and waves. If the sound waves, for example, are received by the ear at a certain rate, the neuron will fire at the same rate, in a sequence of on-off spurts. In this manner, the signal is preserved.

In actuality, however, the process is considerably more complicated. Numerous neurons, sometimes thousands, participate in the transmission of a single input signal. Neurons are very narrow but can vary in length. About 5,000 neurons existing side by side would make a nerve fiber of one inch in diameter. You may note from Fig. 1 that a neuron is comprised of three main parts: the dendrites, the axon, and the cell body which contains the nucleus. The end of the axon branches off into a number of terminal twigs. Nerve impulses travel in only one direction. Sensations are first felt by the dendrite and the signal is passed through the cell body to the axon.

Neurons transmit their electrical impulses to other neurons across a very narrow juncture called a synapse. The human brain contains an estimated 10 to 15 billion neurons. Each has its dendrites, axons, and terminal twigs, hence an inestimable number of synapses. Transmission of the signal across the synapse is a chemical process. Acetylchoiine (Ach) is secreted by the axon. The chemical travels in all directions in spurts, or waves. The wave pattern of the Ach corresponds to the pattern of firing of the neuron. In other words, the representation of the original signal is still retained and transmitted.

Chapter 12 discussed long- and short-term memory. It is believed that short-term memory involves a closed circuit of neurons where electronic signals reverberate (circulate) after the signals have been received from the sensory neurons. In the meantime, the signal tries to cross the synapse to other neurons that are connected to cells of long-term memory.

Referring to Fig. 2, examine what is undoubtedly a greatly simplified illustration of the theory of consolidation. An electronic signal is transmitted along neuron A to the synapse, and from there it is transmitted to neuron B. The two form what is called a reverberating circuit. Neurons C, D, and E at the synaptic juncture have the potential to receive the signal also. It is of the utmost im-

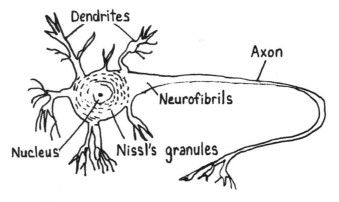

Fig. 1

Neuron

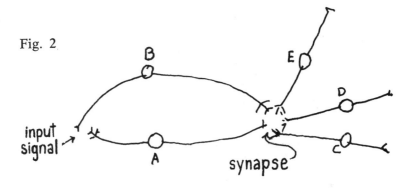

Fig. 2

Theory of Consolidation

portance for an understanding of this subject to know that *transmission of a signal across the synapse does not always occur.* If this were not the case, if the signal were to be picked up by every neuron at a synapse, messages would be sprayed indiscriminately to all parts of the brain. There would be no means by which the messages could be routed and controlled. There would be no means of discriminating, sorting, and selecting relevant data. On the other hand, when the signal does successfully cross the synapse, learning will occur, and consolidation will take place.

What determines receptivity?

Whether the signal will be received by a specific neuron and transmitted to long-term areas, depends upon the state of the synapse, the length of time that the signal is kept reverberating, and the receptivity of that neuron to that particular signal. The state of the synapse depends upon the amount of Ach secreted, which is dependent upon the level of excitement. The more aroused and alert one is, in general, the more Ach that is secreted. Generally speaking, the more Ach secreted at a synapse, the better are the chances that the signal will cross successfully. However, there is a point under conditions of extreme excitement or fear, when too much Ach is secreted, and as a result, the signal is not transmitted properly and in some cases is blocked altogether. Poor mental functioning when you are in a state of panic and anxiety, can be better understood from this standpoint. Apparently, mild excitement is the best condition for neural transmission.

The circuit will continue to be active as long as the mind is thinking about a particular experience or thought. The longer the signal is kept in short-term memory, the more cells that will be affected by the signal. The signal will then have more time to cross the synapse and be transmitted to longer-term areas. That is why repetition aids in retention.

The main question at this point involves the notion of receptivity. What makes a neural cell become receptive to a signal? Why do some neurons accept certain signals and reject other signals?

In a way, the memory signal may be thought of as looking for a place in which to settle. If the input signal has a special meaning for the person, if there is a relationship between what is being presently learned and something that has been learned previously, the reverberating signal will find its way to the cells harboring the prior knowledge. The more relationships a thought has, the more likely it is that its signals will find a place to lodge. Science is still quite hazy on the neuro-biological actions underlying the reasons for this selective receptivity. However, laboratory studies have observed electrical waves passing over the cerebral cortex during learning. In addition, these waves differ in kind with different types of learning. It also has been observed that all cells in the cortex are in a constant state of firing, though their voltage levels are comparatively low. The cells discharge in the form of electrical pulses and these cells then take on a distinctive pattern of discharge. It may then be conjectured that the signal will be received by cells or a group of cells with similar patterns. The neurons which connect these cells with synapses in the short-term area must have some way of feeling and sensing this pattern. They tend to attract signals in short-term memory that have similar frequencies.

This type of reception resembles the reception of radio and television signals. These latter signals are carried through the air at a particular frequency and will only be transmitted to, and received by, the antennas of those sets that are "tuned in" to the correct frequency or channel. Thus, when a radio set is tuned to 500 kilocycles, it will only receive signals at that frequency. All other frequencies will be rejected. The antenna may be thought of as being analogous to the connecting neuron, and the radio may be thought of as being analogous to a group of cells in the long-term area of the brain.

Keep in mind that a multitude of neurons meet at a synapse. Signals have several possible alternatives. Each synapse has its own minute electro-chemical decisions to make. Due to the complex interconnections of axons and dendrites, eight hundred or more neurons may meet at a synaptic juncture. The impulse may cross the synapse or may not. If it does cross the synapse, it will be picked up by one or more neurons. Some of the neurons may connect to memories not related to the author's ideas, and may then trigger a series of unrelated recollections. However, when they are consciously awakened, the cells containing the chemistry of the old knowledge are activated. The cells become more receptive and attract the incoming signal by making the path of connecting neurons more excitable. That is why this book has emphasized such concepts as reading for a purpose, thinking, and hypothesizing while reading or listening.

The concept of consolidation has been greatly simplified in this discussion. There may actually be hundreds or even thousands of synapses or circuits operating in short-term memory, and the connecting neurons take far more complex paths than just indicated, but the basic principles appear to be sound.

What memory is made of

In recalling knowledge and using it for a period of time, you take something from your subconscious mind and bring it to consciousness. In what form has this knowledge actually been between the time it was learned and the moment you use it? Furthermore, you cannot help but marvel at the cohesiveness of stored memories. It is not necessary to remember all events in chronological order should you wish to recall a specific event. You recall events that seem to be undisturbed by other experiences. When you wish to recall something, you can do so without being bombarded by an avalanche of other memories. (Although it is true that other branches of psychology, particularly the study of perception, show that memories, especially those containing an emotional significance, are altered by the dynamics of the personality, the basic experience nevertheless remains cohesive.)

What is the nature of this wondrous storage mechanism? What constitutes storage once the signals reach the cells? Do the cells keep the original representation of the idea by continuing electrical activity? Or is the chemical and physical nature of the cells storing the memories restructured in some way? Due to recent developments, most psychologists support the view that changes take place in the chemistry of the cells. The various chemical changes represent memories when they are in a subconscious or resting state.

The neurons in the brain are surrounded by other cells which do not conduct electrically. They are known as neuroglia, or glia. The glia as well as the neurons contain a chemical called RNA (ribonucleic acid). RNA is similar to DNA (deoxyribonucleic acid), which has been established as the substance within genes that determines hereditary characteristics. In RNA, the genes carry a memory for growth and development. There is a multitude of somewhat inconclusive evidence implicating RNA as an agent of memory. It is found in the nuclei of both neural and glia cells. Its concentration decreases in old age, much as one's memorizing ability does, and it has been reported that RNA supplements in diets of aged persons improve their memory.

Possibly the most dramatic experiment on this subject was performed on albino rats. Two groups of rats were trained to approach a food cup and obtain a food pellet when a stimulus was presented. The stimulus for one group was a flashing light; the other group responded to a clicking sound. The rats were then killed. RNA was extracted from their brains and injected into rats that had never been exposed to either situation. Six of the eight "click injected" rats responded to the click, and seven of the eight "light injected" rats responded only to the light. Other experiments of this type have been conducted with similar results.

RNA is a very long molecule which contains chains of four base chemicals. These bases may appear in any order. The sequential order seems to be a code containing representations of experiences (knowledge and memory). In an experiment to examine the connection between RNA and knowledge, young rats were trained to walk a tightrope in order to reach food on a platform. After they had learned to perform the feat well, they were killed. Other rats, which had not been trained, were killed also. The scientists then examined the nerve cells which are associated with recognition-of-balance cues. The results showed significant differences in the sequential order of the bases between the RNA of the experimental group and the RNA of the control groups. In addition, the order of bases in the RNA molecules of the experimental group was distinctly similar. Since RNA contains chains of four bases which can be arranged in any order, if one molecule is about 4,000 bases long, the number of different combinations of the RNA bases would be 4^{4000}. Multiply this number by the billions of neural and glia cells in the brain and you can imagine the fantastic amount of information that the brain has the capacity to store. Of course, we do not know the code as yet or exactly what constitutes a unit of information.

One drawback prevented acceptance of the RNA theory. The level of RNA in a cell involved in learning had been shown to build up to a peak shortly after the learning experience, but then gradually subside, so that it was back to normal level after about 24 hours. Since memories can exist for far longer than 24 hours, it seemed questionable that RNA was the actual memory molecule.

Scientists now think that the function of RNA is to direct the assembly of the protein structure in the cells. RNA permanently alters the structure of the cells, but the memory is retained over a long period due to the protein formation of the cells.

A brilliant experiment on this subject was conducted by George Ungar and Wolfgang Parr. Rats who normally like the dark were given a shock each time they approached a dark place. Eventually, as a consequence, they were taught fear of the dark. A broth made out of their brain tissue was injected into rats and white mice that had not been taught this fear. Afterward, those injected rats and mice also avoided darkness. After experimenting further and chemically analyzing the brain extracts, it was believed that one particular sequence of amino acids (a protein is comprised of amino acids), was responsible for the association of darkness and shock. To check this hypothesis, the substance was duplicated, not from brain extracts, but from laboratory chemicals. Again, the injected animals showed fear of the dark. Thus, for the first time, people gained some insight into the chemical code in which memory is stored.

The code in itself consists of more than just the original input representation. It is far more complicated than that. By the time a signal reaches long-term storage, it has become integrated with signals from other cells in the brain and the result is a mixture. When two or more cells combine signals, new chemical structures are created, forming the physical basis of learning and the formation of associations. An association is probably formed when two bits of information are found in the same cell.

Conclusion

It has been said that the more one learns, the more one becomes conscious of one's own ignorance. This certainly holds true in the study of memory. We still have very little idea of the method used by cells to transform electrical impulses into chemical codes; we know only that RNA and the protein structures of cells are involved.

Retrieving the signals

The process known as recall involves a mechanism similar to that for storing information. Both are basically accomplished by neurons, synapses, and cellular chemicals. How this reverse process works, though, is not known. We can only assume that there is some means by which the stored chemical knowledge is tapped, and that it reverts back to electrical impulses, and finally to the actual images and verbal reproductions that make up our conscious thought. It is possible that our conscious thought involves a duplication of a short- and long-term memory system, but in reverse. The localization theory suggests that memories are stored in various parts of the brain. The short-term circuit in recall serves to hold signals that attract similar signals from the diverse areas of the cortex. There they are integrated into thought.

More is being learned each day, and a greater knowledge of the recall process appears certain in the near future. We have made great strides since the days when the concept of mind involved an explanation relying on the supernatural. We know that the mind is capable of storing voluminous information in our waking state, and that it sorts out segments of this information for long-term storage. Most important of all, we now know enough to gain some concepts from physiology that can be referred to in respect to memory improvement. Improving memory consists first of using those techniques that will facilitate the process of consolidation, and second, in using those techniques that will help your mind locate the knowledge when you want to retrieve it. A good way to review the principles in this book is to imagine how each technique in turn will, from a physiological standpoint, aid memory.

CHAPTER 17

how to get others to remember your ideas

In a multitude of situations you probably find yourself becoming exasperated when others do not remember your instructions, requests, birthday, the benefits of your product, and many, many other pieces of information. At today's fast-moving pace, the effective communication of ideas becomes ever more important. In communicating, you wish an individual or group will remember to perform a certain action, or you wish an individual or group will in turn pass on your words and thoughts to others. For information to be successfully communicated, two things must happen—one, the information must be expressed and transmitted by the sender; and two, the information must be remembered by the receiver. This chapter will show how you can use the principles of memory to assure retention of your ideas so that successful communication may occur.

A while ago my wife and I were greatly concerned about our two-year-old boy. He just loved to run out in the street. The street is greatly travelled; we knew the danger and tried everything from pleading to spanking to keep him from running out, but all was in vain. It probably did not take him long to learn that he should not play in the street, but like so many of us, he would forget what he was supposed to do when seized with an irresistible temptation.

One Saturday night, a baby-sitter arrived so that my wife and I could go out for dinner. She brought with her a copy of "Mad Magazine." I picked it up and looked at the back cover, which had a very funny cartoon of a man walking across the street, being hit by a car, and the pedestrian signal, instead of spelling "WALK" or "DON'T WALK," spelled "SUE." The picture of the man as he was being hit by the car was grossly exaggerated and absurdly contorted. At that moment a plan for successful communication evolved in my mind. I told my son that I was going to tell him a story. I went into the story in depth—meaning that I emphasized all the gory details. I pointed out all the different parts of the body being "messed up" by the "terrible crash." I then asked him to think about what it would be like if a car hit *him*.

147

Awful, you think? A child shouldn't be exposed to blood at a tender age? I shouldn't be exposed to blood before dinner? I will combat opinion with fact. Afterward, he would not go out in the street for the largest candy bar in the world. I can only imagine the vision of that terrible accident that flashed through his mind whenever he looked at the street.

What enabled me to get through to him? I made the thought of his being hit by a car, and the consequent pain, into an *emotional experience* for him. Furthermore, I didn't just tell him what could happen. I showed him. He was then able to place a *visual image* of the event in his memory, and the visual image always makes a powerful impression, especially on children.

Can the above principles be used to communicate information to adults as well? Of course, and so can all of the other principles in Chapter 2. This section examines four areas in which these principles can be applied. You should try to transfer these suggestions to your own unique situation.

The teacher

A teacher or instructor is probably in the best position to utilize principles of memory. This book should reinforce any teacher-training courses that extol the benefits of visual aids and auxiliary materials. Compared to words, pictures and objects are easier for pupils *of any age* to concentrate on and remember.

Most school teachers tend to stay away from technical subjects. It is easy to present a history lesson describing what happened first, second, and so on, but technical material takes more organization if the subject is to be understood. Comprehension will be facilitated if the teacher gives an overview of the subject beforehand. If the objective of a lesson is to teach how a certain machine works, the instructor should first illustrate the purpose of the machine and then the basic principle upon which it operates. When these are firmly fixed in the pupils' minds, all else falls into place.

The teacher can and should utilize all of the principles in this book, such as reviewing periodically, helping students pinpoint the important parts of a lesson, and getting students to speak and write about what they know. The teacher is also in a position to assure the utilization of the most effective principle of all—usage. At every opportunity the pupil should be shown how knowledge of the subject can be helpful in his/her own life.

The salesperson

Ideally, a salesperson wishes to sell his/her product directly to the buyer. In the selling of insurance plans, cosmetics, vacuum cleaners, and a host of other items, communication is a direct appeal to action. However, for the sale of many more expensive products to large corporations or institutions, the sale must be first made to an administrator who is responsible for presenting an evaluation of the salesperson's product to his/her superiors. Whether or not a sale will be made under these circumstances depends to a large extent on how well the administrator remembers the benefits derived from the product.

I started in the field of learning by selling Rapid Reading courses to schools. The usual procedure was first to see the school principal, who might or might not have the power to give a go-ahead. In one of my first appointments, the assistant principal came down, explaining that the principal had a sudden emergency. So here was a situation where I had to present my program to the assistant who I expected would present the program favorably to the principal who would present the program to the superintendent who would present it to the Board of Education.

Normally, whenever information is communicated verbally, the content of the information decreases both quantitatively and qualitatively. Had I been older and wiser, I would have developed my own sudden emergency and left with a minimum of time and energy wasted. I went through my presentation beautifully, however. He said it all sounded very good and he would tell the principal about it. I left happily, not knowing that I did not have a ghost of a chance of making that sale.

You, the salesperson, must remember that these middlemen are not as motivated as you are to present the information, simply because they are not paid directly to speak about your product. Yet selling to these people can be accomplished (as long as there is only one in-between person to deal with), by helping his/her retention and recall. You can aid retention by asking questions. For example, I would divide my product, a memory course, into three categories. I would first ask the person if he/she feels as though my program will benefit the employees. After an affirmative response, I would ask how he/she feels about our references. Then I would request his/her thoughts on our price. These questions help in a multitude of ways.

In answering these questions, he/she *organizes* the presentation into three major areas and that will certainly help retention. Responding to these questions makes him/her recall other portions of the presentation, such as who the references were and how my price compares with others in the field. And last but not least, as the person speaks favorably about the program, he/she will remember *his/her own words*.

You should never refrain from asking questions such as these because you fear a negative answer. Look at it this way: By this point in the presentation, he/she personally should be sold.

The problem is to make sure the person remembers, and has the same feelings about the product when he/she must relate the information to others. If the person is not sold at this point—if his/her answer to these questions is negative, you're not going to make the sale anyway. On the other hand, if his/her answer to one of the questions is undecided, then the questions have been of great value because you now know what areas should be reinforced with more sales material.

A successful salesperson I know uses another excellent technique. He states at the beginning of his presentation, "Now, you know your business better than I, so I'm not going to tell you how this computer system will help. What I'll do is simply go over the benefits of our system, and perhaps you will be able to see where it would be helpful." This challenges his listener, who is more likely to think positively; the listener will remember *his/her own thoughts*, and will *value* his/her own thoughts.

Visual sales material is also helpful for the same reasons mentioned earlier. If the material is in the form of a brochure of some type, you should let the listener turn the pages. This will enhance his/her concentration. Allowing the customer to turn the pages will also bring his/her own physical movements into play and that enhances retention. If you are a car salesman, it is imperative that the prospective customer get into the car and drive it. Later, when the customer is more serious about buying, the remembered experience will be a subconscious motivating force.

The public speaker

Research studies have indicated that in a lecture or public speaking type of situation, less than 25 percent of the speaker's ideas are remembered. At first I thought that statistic incredible, yet in many circumstances it is probably true and understandable. In speaking to a large audience, there is little or no eye contact, no direct questions, no personal involvement on the part of the speaker. As a result, the speaker must be content to realize that less information will be transmitted to listeners, for a given unit of time. This means that more words than would appear necessary must be spent in summarizing and restating the main points.

A speaker should help the listener *prepare to receive information* by stating objectives—the ideas he/she expects to put across—as early in the speech as possible. He/she then should take greater than normal measures to be sure that he/she shows how each of the points in the speech relates to the objectives. Any divergence from the stated objectives or overall theme will cause *interference*. Statements such as "That all reminds me of the time when . . ." may lead to an amusing anecdote but it had definitely better relate reasonably well to the main theme. Otherwise, the anecdote may be remembered and the speech forgotten.

I said earlier that emotional involvement aided the retention of ideas in children, and so it is with adults. People will remember their feelings above all else. We have all seen speakers who are very poorly organized, but if they are riding the crest of a strong emotional tide that also sweeps over the listeners, they get away with any sort of ranting and raving, and the listeners will remember.

One of the best techniques to get the audience involved emotionally is to replace statistics with personal experiences, or story content about one particular person. The story of a single family's ordeal following a flood will do more for memory than a bunch of statistics telling how much property damage was caused by floods last year. People do not identify with numbers but they do identify with other people. A speech should provide a total experience. If you give the listeners only words, they will have only words to remember. If, however, you communicate with gesture, actions, and voice inflections, this will not only elicit emotional response, but will also store more memories in the brains of the listeners.

Interpersonal communication

Roy Garn in his book, *The Power of Emotional Appeal*, made some very interesting and true statements. He said, "All speaking is public speaking." All the suggestions made in the preceding section hold true whether speaking to a group or an individual. A single listener is subject to the same principles of organization. The more quickly you come to the point in a lengthy dissertation, the more that will be absorbed overall.

A person in interpersonal communication, Mr. Garn said, is able to experience a greater variety of emotional responses than when this same person is part of a group. Reaching a person's emotions will aid his/her retention, of course, but all individuals react differently. People show a tremendous variety of emotional responses to any given set of circumstances. The variations are caused by the unique psychological makeup of each individual. Mr. Garn went further to state that each individual responds emotionally to certain stimuli. We all have a certain emotional soft spot. When you know what the soft spot of your listener is, whether it be money, romance, self-preservation, or recognition, you can communicate more effectively using statements that tap the soft spot.

Helping people *discriminate* is always beneficial. A department manager can use this type of effective statement: "Bill, what do you think is the *most important* feature of this plan?" A variation of this statement could be used just as easily by a sales-person.

Numbers are difficult unless a little *thought* is added. I once asked a secretary just before I left the office to call number 3342. Noting the hectic surrounding circumstances, and knowing that particular secretary, I decided to go further. "Hey, did you know that 3342 B.C. is the year the sphinx was built in Egypt?" I said. "How interesting," she sighed. Well, maybe it wasn't interesting or even true, but she remembered.

Do you want people to stop forgetting your birthday? It's no problem if you relate a thought to it. You can add a meaning-ful statement to any date of any month. If you were born on July 4, or January 1, or October 12, there would not be any difficulty. Why not stretch the utilization of these dates a little by telling people you were born two days before Christmas or three days after the begin-ning of Spring? If this cannot be done, then relate your birthday to some scheduled event—the start of the world series, election day, etc. If you still cannot find a suitable relationship, look into an almanac and find the most significant event in history that happened on your day. Every day has some historical significance. Some people may still forget the exact date, but they will not forget the event.

using memories
for success

The ultimate goal in studying memory is self-improvement. The more one learns, the more one gains an appreciation of the enormous complexities of the human organism. Memory is intricately interwoven with other psychological functions, including many areas of self-improvement. One area is personality. With this in mind, this section turns your attention beyond the world of books.

One can easily observe great individual differences in people's abilities to learn and perform acts involving muscular control. Even within an individual, the ability to recall motor activities varies enormously with the type of activity. One person may learn and improve in tennis at a remarkable rate, be only fair at learning to type, and be completely hopeless on the dance floor, no matter how much instruction he/she receives.

Personal
Elements Affecting
Memory

When you practice something, the repetition refines the neural pathways going from the muscles being used to the part of the brain that contains the memories for the performance of the skill. It would be reasonable to expect that, to the muscles and nerves, the type of activity being engaged in would make absolutely no difference. Learning one skill would be no more difficult and no easier than learning another. Psychological factors, therefore, must partially account for the disparities.

Perception

Have you ever noticed how two people can view exactly the same event and have completely different stories as to what occurred? Or perhaps you have been anxiously awaiting the arrival of some important person and noticed how slowly the time seemed to pass? These are both examples of the psychological phenomenon of *perception*. How something appears to an individual depends not merely on the actual or real characteristics. Within a person's psychological makeup is the fascinating ability to alter reality so that an object, person, or event has a somewhat different appearance. This is a perception.

Self concept and memory

Beliefs about the self are formed by one's memories of past experiences. Memories of success or failure can cause the person to declare, "I am a good athlete," or, "I am a poor dancer," as well as affecting confidence in a multitude of scholastic, social, and occupational areas. How these memories are constructed, the form that they take, depends on two factors, and there is more of a difference between them than meets the eye. First are the actual experiences a person has had. Second, and of far more importance, is how these experiences are remembered. One student may receive a grade of 80 on a test and remember it as a success. Another may receive the same grade and remember it as just the opposite.

The ratio of past successes to past failures is not the crucial factor determining present behavior, just as sheer amount of reading is not the crucial factor in determining present knowledge. Just as steps must be taken to assure retention of reading material, steps must also be taken to remember experiences. If unsuccessful experiences are reviewed and brooded over, or if they are constantly associated with reflections such as, "If only I had done such and such, it would be different now," these memories will surely become firmly entrenched. Another magnificent way to assure retention of past failures is to organize experiences into a broad inclusive framework. Generalized statements such as "I guess all this shows that I'm just plain dumb," will work wonders in increasing the power of these memories and in weakening confidence.

Thomas Edison was one of many great men who had hundreds of unsuccessful attempts for every success. But it is only the success that everyone remembers. Though differing in proportionate amounts, we all have in our histories successes and failures. However, the successful person habitually remembers his/her *successes*, while the failure habitually remembers his/her *mistakes and losses*. That is why, generally speaking, successful individuals continue to do well while failure leads to more failure.

If a person perceives a given situation as being more difficult than others think it ought to be, considering the person's mental and physical characteristics, he/she is said to be lacking in confidence as far as that particular situation is concerned. A low level of confidence will cause a correspondingly poor use of your abilities, while a high level of confidence will enable you to make full use of your abilities.

A group of engineers were asked to recall as many happy memories as they could. It was found that those who recalled the most were the most successful on the job. You can change the pattern, however, by forgetting about the mistakes and making a determined effort to remember your happy and successful experiences. This is not to say that successful people actually forget their bad experiences. They do not. However, they interpret and store the experience in a different way. They see an unsuccessful attempt as part of a learning process, not as a failure.

Affecting change in your memory systems

A startling experiment has shown how affecting memory can change performance. Two groups of fourth graders were equal in scholastic ability. The children in one group were asked to describe the saddest event in their lives, the children in the other group were to describe their happiest memory. Immediately afterwards, all the pupils were tested in writing a composition. The "happy" group's graded papers were significantly superior.

You should get into the habit of remembering success immediately, and reviewing these memories whenever a situation may seem threatening. If you do not know where to begin, you may start by asking yourself these questions and then answering them: What was your happiest moment? What was the happiest period of your life? Why? What was your greatest achievement? When and how did you conduct yourself in situations causing you to be proud of yourself? Then write these experiences down. Make a long list. Anything will count as long as it gives you a feeling of pride and satisfaction. Anything, from learning to ride a bicycle to being congratulated for helping someone with the dishes. Writing will make these happy memories more likely to be a part of, and to influence, your thoughts in the present and future.

Whenever you are approaching a threatening situation, use your memories to bolster your confidence and maintain a successful attitude. As you approach the boss's office to ask for a raise, recall as many instances as possible in which you spoke forcefully and convincingly, and in which you were successful. Be sure to recapture the full feeling of your accomplishment; feel a sense of pride. If you remember your successes in the past, you will more likely remember to act in the way you would like to act in the future. Always set reasonable goals, slightly higher than your past achievement, and remember your successes.

1. Does memory ability get worse as you get older?

All physical abilities decrease as you get older. Since the brain is a part of the body, it would be less than honest to deny that some loss in mental power does occur. However: One, the mental loss is nowhere near as rapid as the physical. Two, the manner in which you process information will remain as the most important factor in memory at any age, and three, you can slow down the deterioration process significantly by keeping yourself mentally active and alert.

Last but not least, you must consider your perspective. You are comparing your memory now with, say, twenty years ago, when the world was not as complex as it is today. This is an unfair comparison. The age of technology has grown quite rapidly, yet you can easily fail to notice it. There is so much more to learn and remember these days. So much more is being printed. Every trade or career field has its own technical journal. Most of us meet many more people than we did in the past.

Consider the case of a young man who grew up in a small farming town, where practically all of his personal interactions were with a relatively small number of people. He had little trouble learning what sort of behavior was appropriate since the people he came in contact with possessed similar backgrounds and followed traditional mores and customs. The very pace of life was easier and slower. Twenty years later he is in the suburbs of a metropolitan area, married, with children, has many more decisions to make, comes into contact with many more people, all of whom come from differing backgrounds and cultures. The clock is an important part of his life. Is it fair that this man should compare his memory now with the way it was twenty years ago?

Although all our lives are affected in different ways, the environment has changed, and we are all affected by it to some degree. You thus must consider this perspective when you say that your memory has deteriorated with age. It may only appear that way because your life and the world around you have changed.

2. I keep seeing an advertisement for a program which promises to show how you can quickly and easily develop a phenomenal, photographic-type memory. Among some more wild claims, they say that if I act now, while the supply lasts, I will receive their secrets for half price. Do you think they may have something worthwhile?

With many of these offers, if you are "lucky" enough to respond before the supply runs out, you receive a small booklet which contains nothing that has not been covered in this, as well as other books on memory. There are no miracles, no quick and easy answers, in any area of self improvement. Improving memory and concentration is like improving anything else. First it takes knowledge. Then it takes forethought, imagination, and practice.

I believe that acquiring knowledge in areas of self improvement, whether it be rapid reading, creative writing, memory, speaking, or whatever, is extremely worthwhile. Nevertheless, I would like to suggest two caveats when it comes to investing in these areas. One, don't pay an abnormally high price, and two, don't expect any immediate and easy "secrets" to success.

3. Does mental exercise help memory and concentration?

Concentration does improve, as stated earlier, when you get more in the habit of focusing attention in daily activities, or through planned exercises such as meditation. The way to improve memory cannot be so simply stated. Experiments were conducted on students to test the effect of practicing the memorization of non-sensical words, on retention in unrelated areas. The results showed neither harmful nor beneficial effects.

Rote memorization exercised alone appears to have little, if any, value. Mental activity in general, however, does keep the mind alert and healthy. One seventy-five-year-old bridge-playing, well read woman was one of the best memory pupils I've ever had.

Rote memorization may have no beneficial effects, but practice and exercise in using the techniques and principles discussed here definitely will enhance proficiency which will, in turn, help memory. Practice and exercise will enable you to form associations more fluidly and quickly. The more you practice reading with the proper techniques in mind, the more easily you will grasp the author's organizational structure. Exercising can aid in improving the ability to see relationships, recognize categories, make selections, and so on.

4. Is the study of memory related to extrasensory perception in any way?

The question assumes the existence of ESP, though it has not yet been completely proven. Nevertheless a relationship can be observed. Those who have had what they feel is a psychic experience, report that the sensations occurred during periods of high emotion or complete relaxation, both being conditions which enhance memory. Furthermore, telepathic messages seem to be received through visual channels. These observations hold up with remarkable consistency. You have seen how effective using visual imagery is in memory. Does this mean that improving visual abilities will improve psychic abilities? I really don't know, but several people knowledgeable in the field of parapsychology will answer that question affirmatively.

5. How much forgetting is due to the unconscious act of repression?

Repression is a term used by psychoanalysts to denote the unconscious process by which the mind selectively blocks certain events or thoughts from being available for recall. The events or thoughts repressed are associated with guilt or fear on the part of the subject. Repression is said to begin in early childhood, but the apparent loss of memory can be explained in other ways. From a practical standpoint, I hardly believe this phenomenon accounts for much forgetting. We remember moments when we felt guilt or anxiety, as well as remembering happier moments.

6. Is intelligence related to concentration and memory?

Those who score high on I.Q. tests generally show high scores on tests measuring the ability to concentrate. The two appear to be closely related. Notice the words "ability to concentrate." In other words, poor concentration does not mean low intelligence. Numerous other factors such as interest, habit, and emotions all determine the degree of concentration.

Memory, surprisingly, has considerably less of a relationship to intelligence. Intelligence is basically the ability to learn, and therefore an intelligent person will learn more and remember more. But once something is learned, the ability to retain is not related to intelligence. Apes have been known to remember a sequence of 30 actions in order to obtain a food pellet. It took longer to get these actions into memory, of course, but once learned, they were not easily forgotten.

7. Can substances I eat or drink affect memory?

Health and blood circulation to the brain are a factor in memory, particularly in later years. Generally the same foods that are harmful to health will eventually hamper mental functioning. Fatty substances can leave deposits in arteries, causing poor circulation. Overly restrictive diets, on the other hand, can cause the death of brain cells. Wheat germ is one of the best sources of vitamin E, which facilitates blood flow. For more detail on this subject, I would recommend one of the Adelle Davis books.

One of the most harmful substances known, from the standpoint of the physiology of memory, is alcohol. With every "high," you experience the sensation of brain cells dying. These cells can never be replaced. You have billions of brain cells, so a few cocktails occasionally won't matter much from a practical standpoint. However, habitual or excessive indulgence will eventually take its toll. Examinations of the brains of alcoholics at autopsies showed the brains to be shrunken or atrophied. I'm not participating in any moral causes—just stating facts.

Certain drugs, such as amphetamines, improve learning ability, but they have unpleasant and harmful side effects. The best suggestion is to avoid them. Your brain has all the chemicals it needs if you use it properly.

8. *I find myself being reluctant to use the association technique because I always seem to come up with ludicrous, insulting, or violent visions. I'm wondering if it is mentally dangerous to use that technique too often.*

Do not hamper your creativity. Be assured it is perfectly harmless. Your normal thought processes will not be affected by the association technique. Your wild, or violent visions will not be enacted. But if what you visualize *does eventually happen*—then don't do it anymore!

Concluding Statement

By now, you can see that improving memory and concentration requires forethought, practice, and imagination. It is my hope that you will find the principles, methods, and techniques in this book to be of practical value in your everyday life. By giving the reasons for forgetting, the basic principles of memory, and the chapter on physiology, I endeavored to show the "why" as well as the "how" behind the approach.

Yet for this book to attain its ultimate value, you need more than knowledge of the reasons and methods to improve memory and concentration. You should not end your knowledge and skills here, but instead should extend and develop them throughout life. I wish you success in this endeavor. I hope you will also find it fun!

Index